AWESOME MAZES FOR KIDS

Want a freebie?
Sign up to our VIP newsletter and
we'll send you something cool!

www.pixelpassage.net/vip

Maze 1

Maze 2

Maze 3

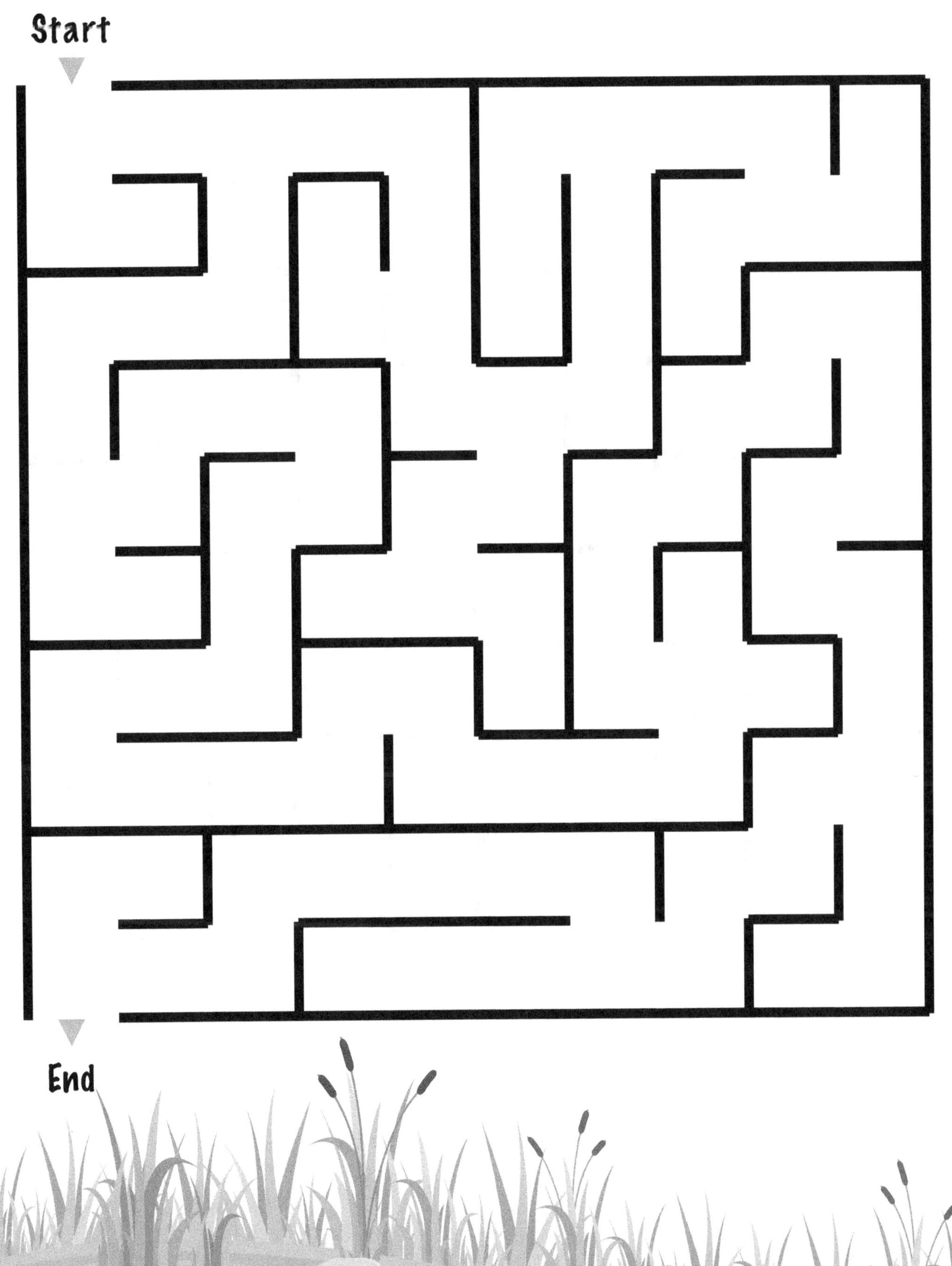

Maze 4

Maze 5

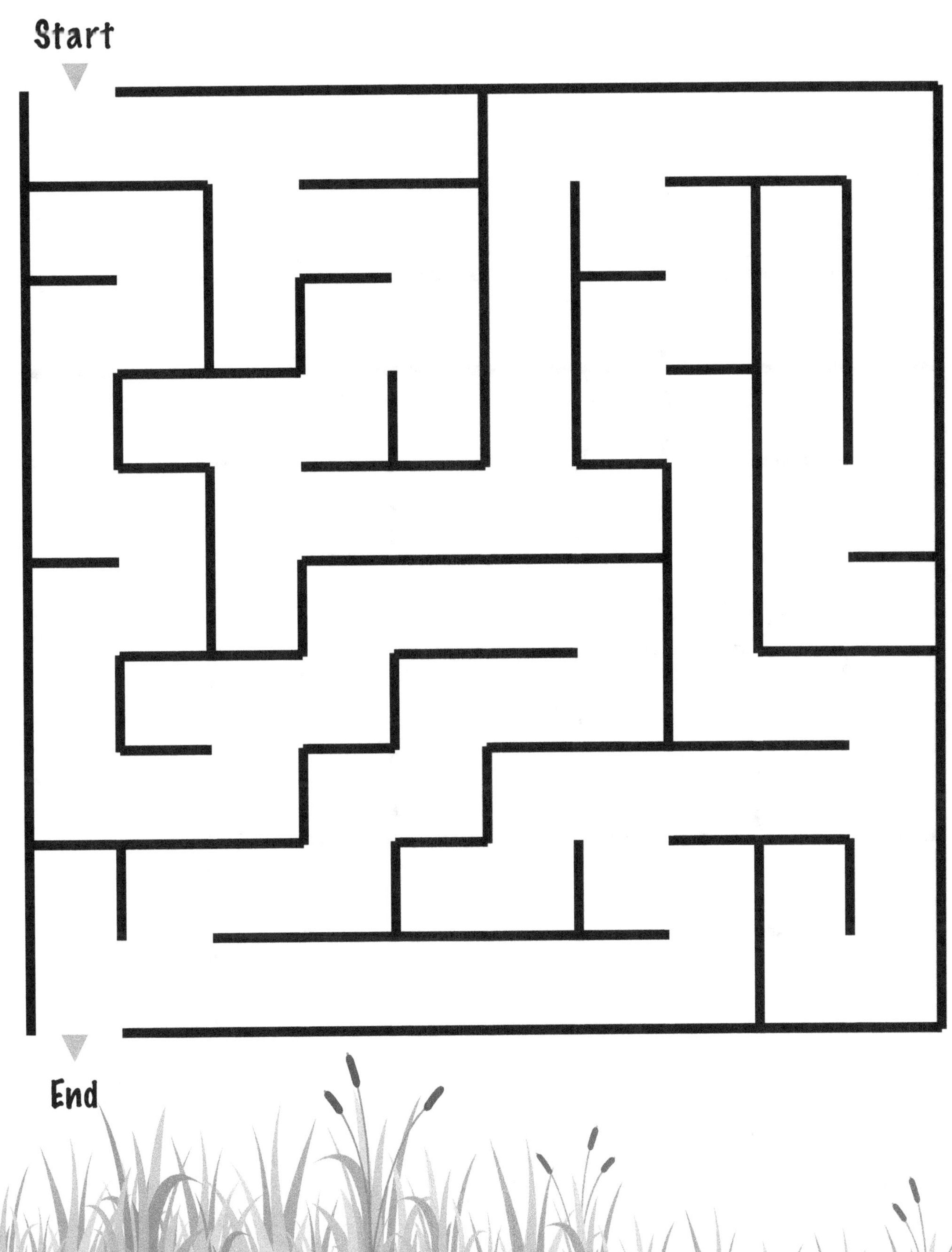

Maze 6

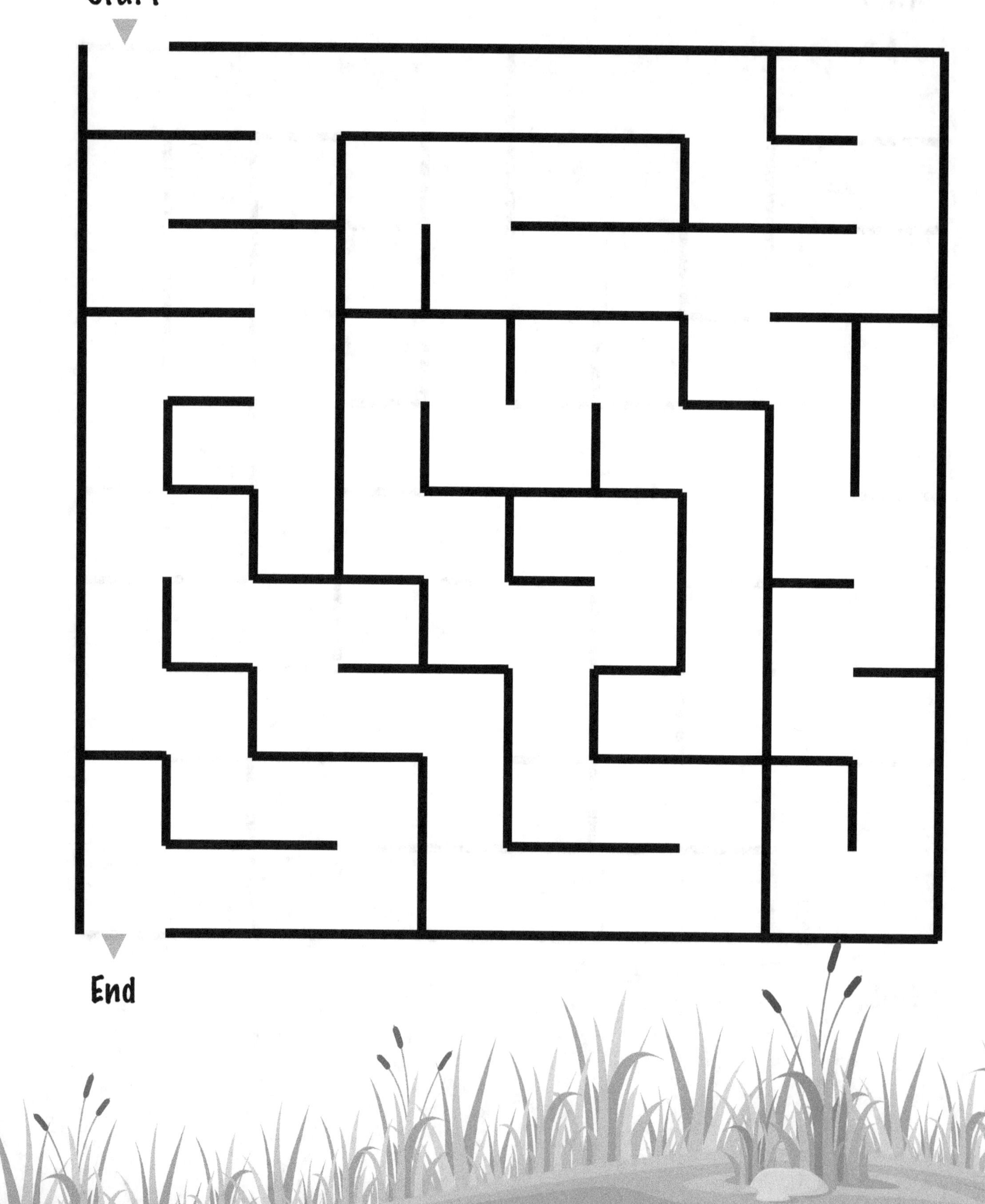

Maze 7

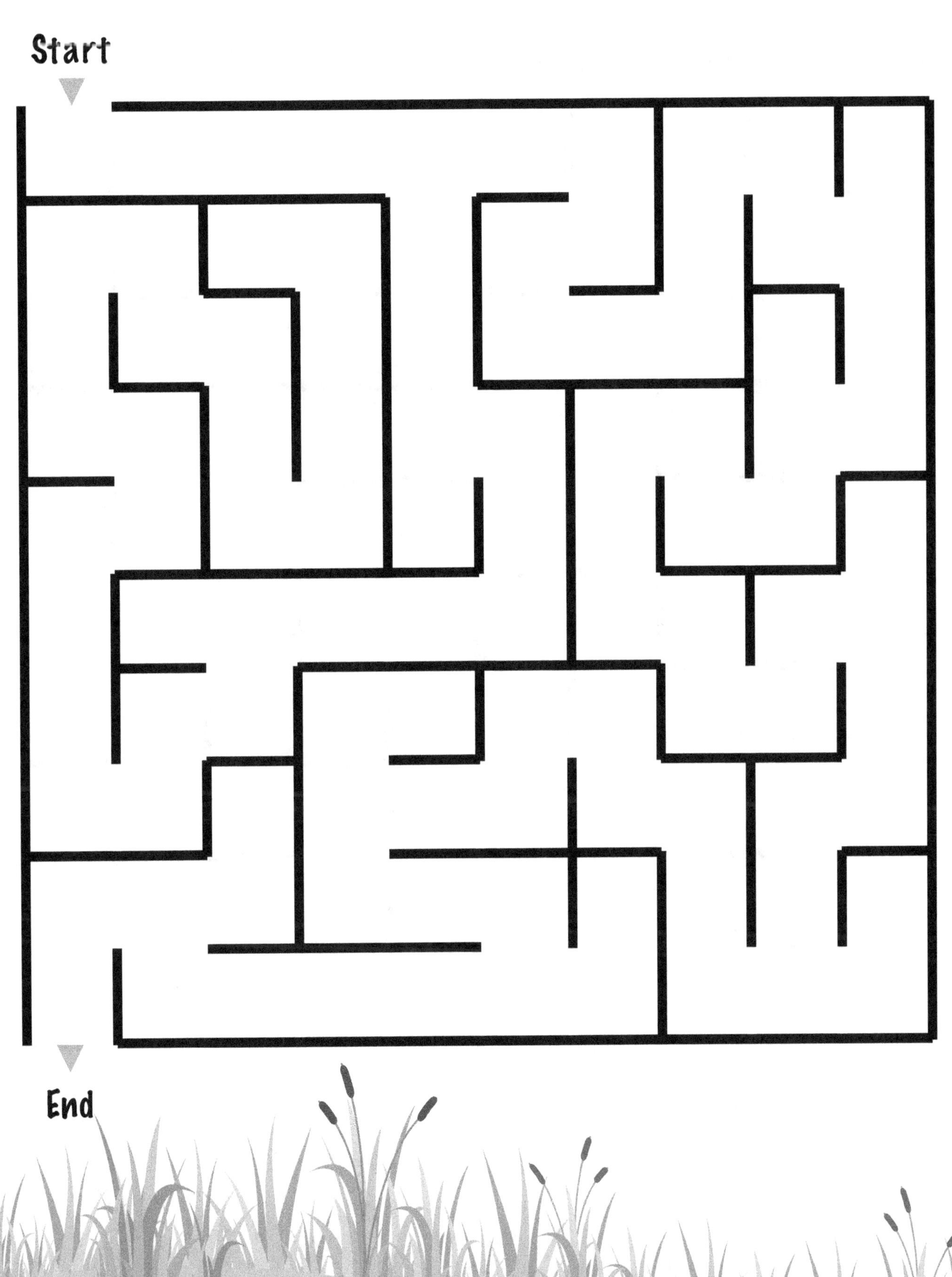

Maze 8

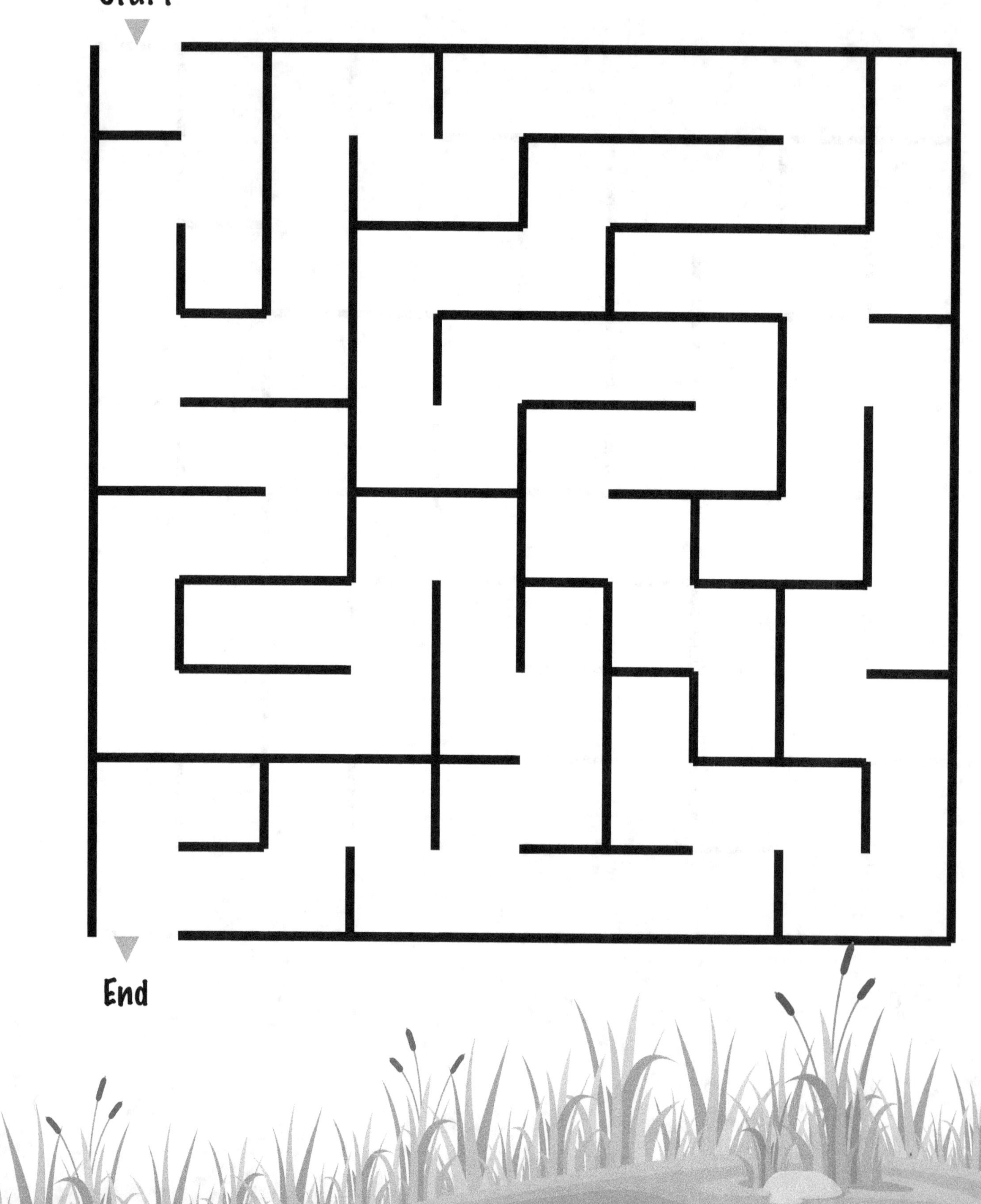

Maze 9

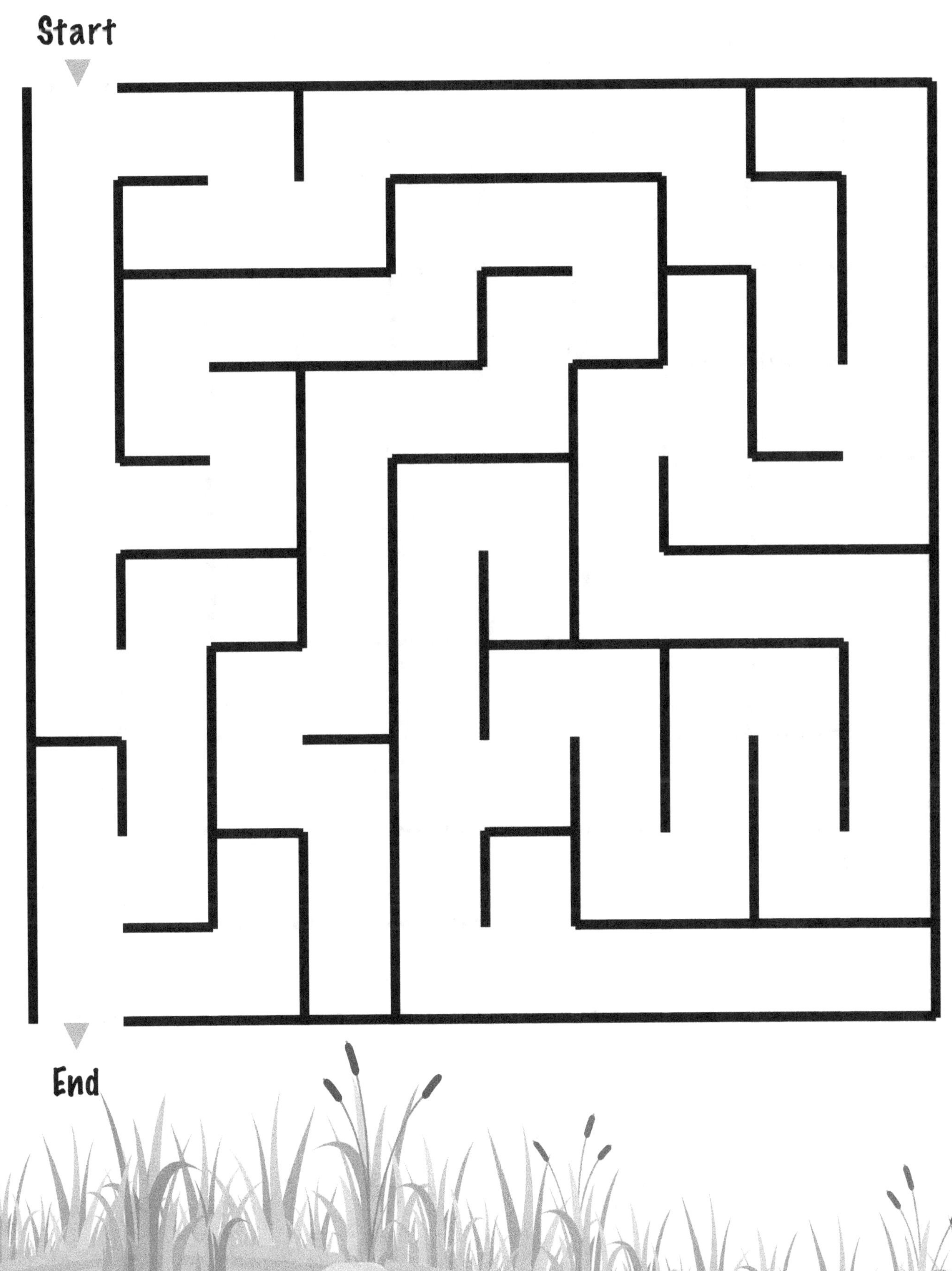

Maze 10

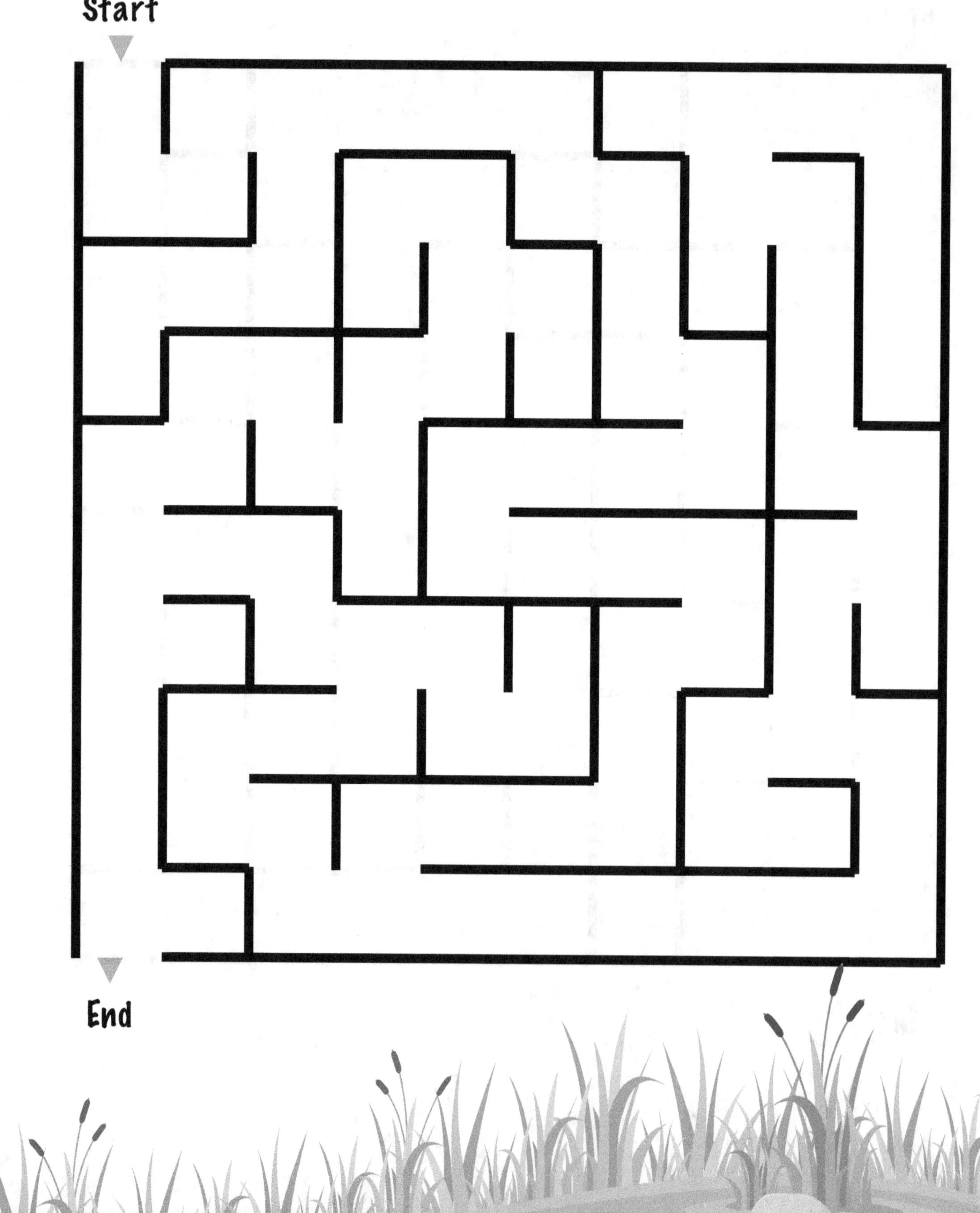

Maze 11

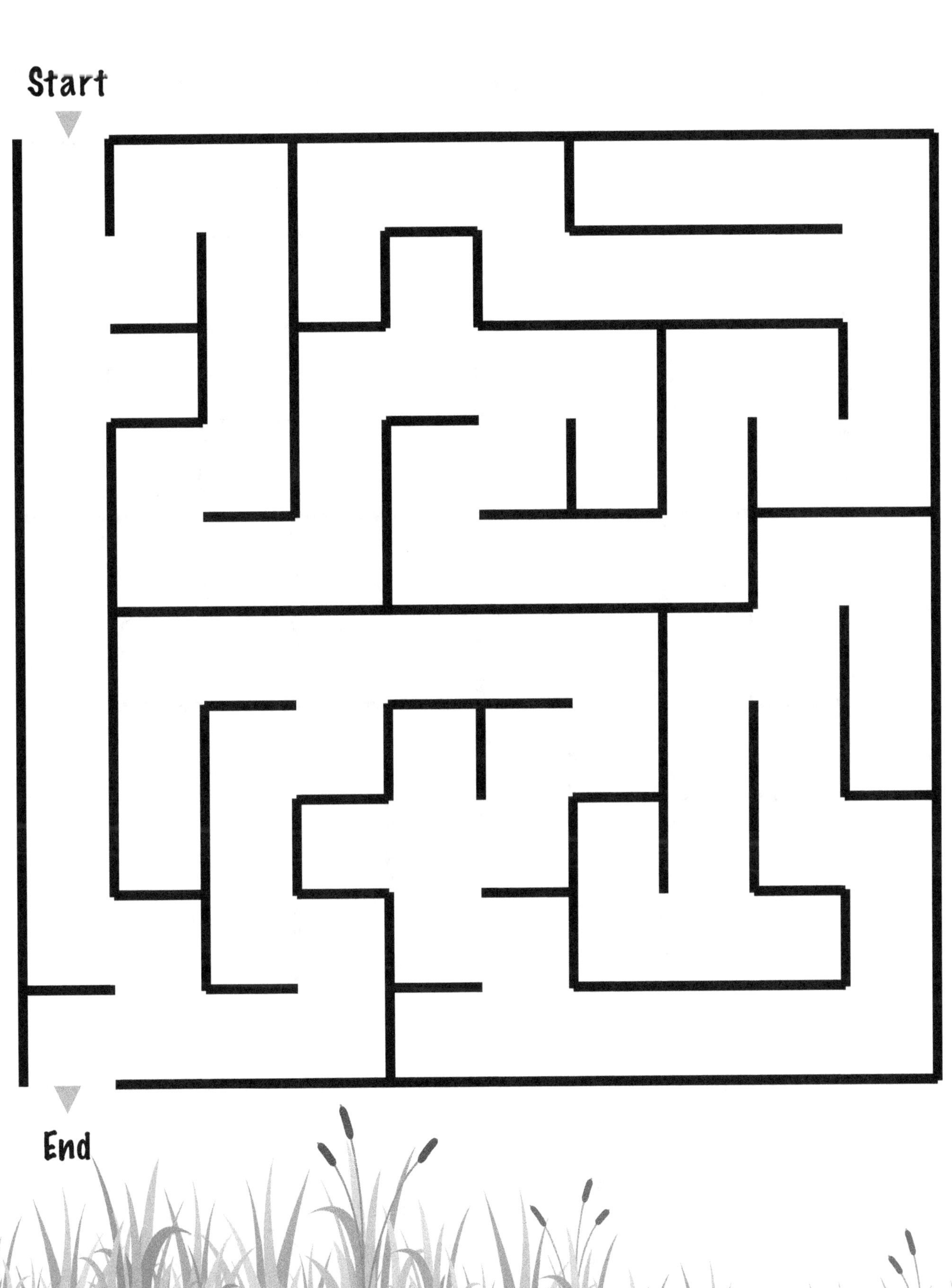

Maze 12

Maze 13

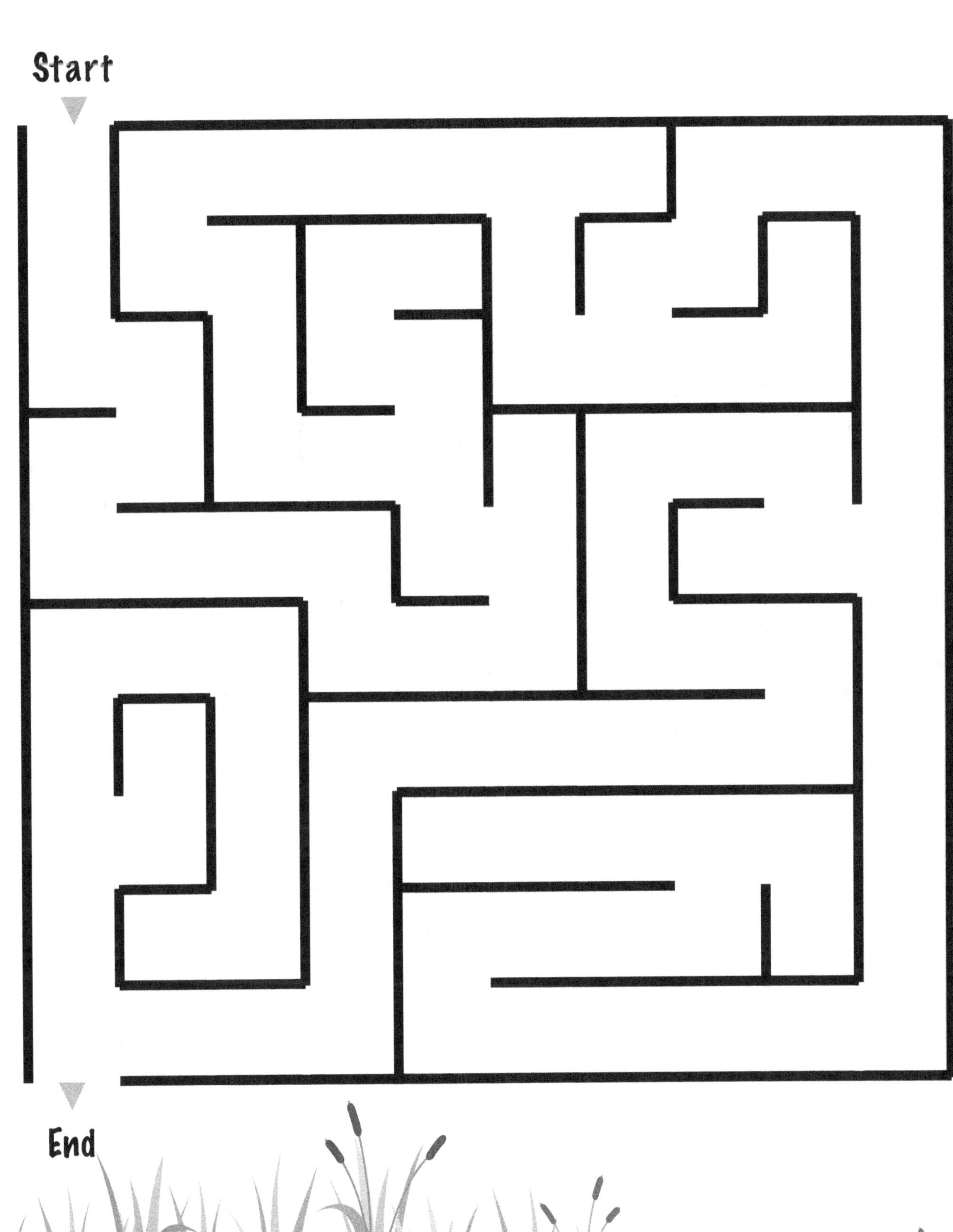

Maze 14

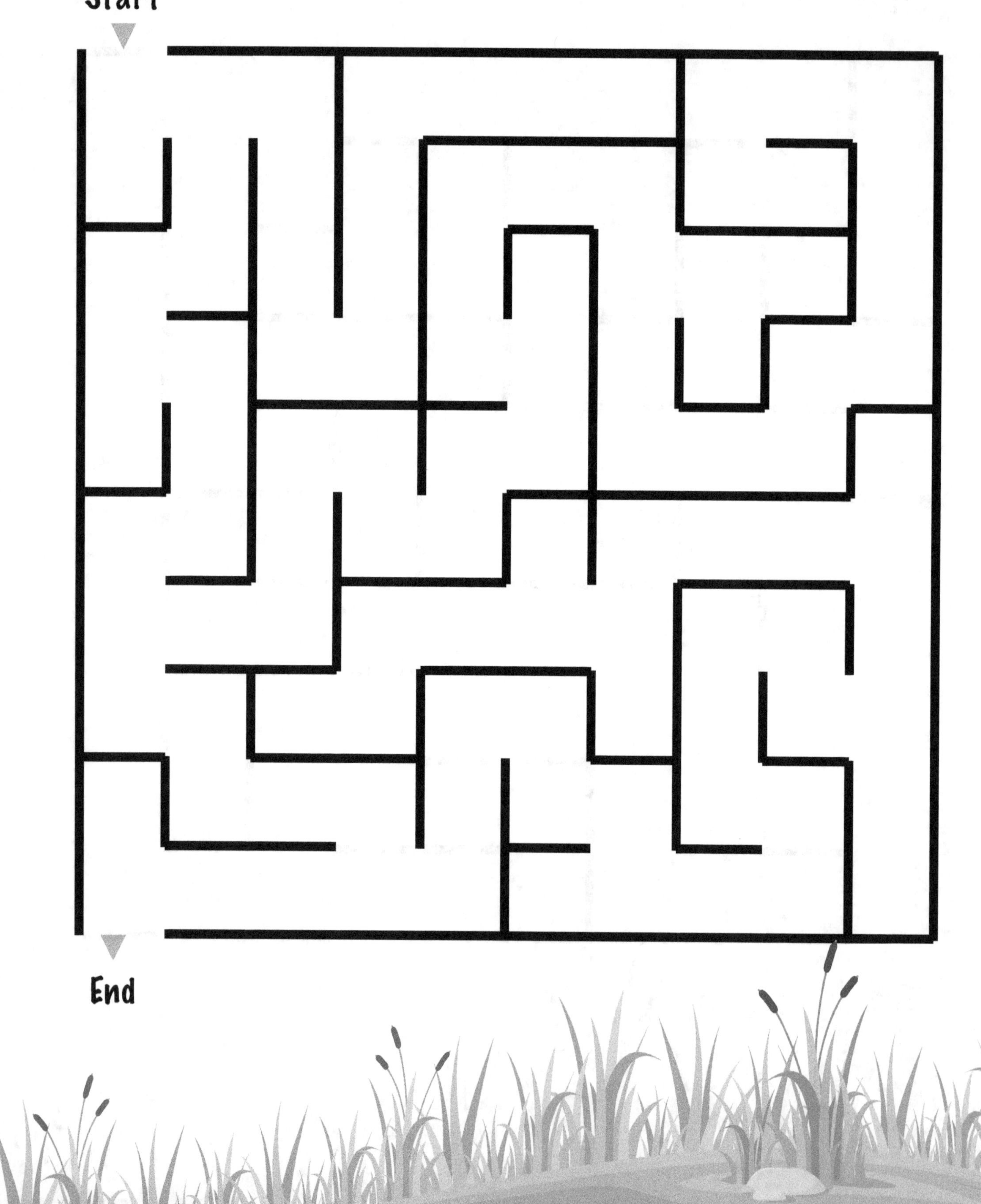

Maze 15

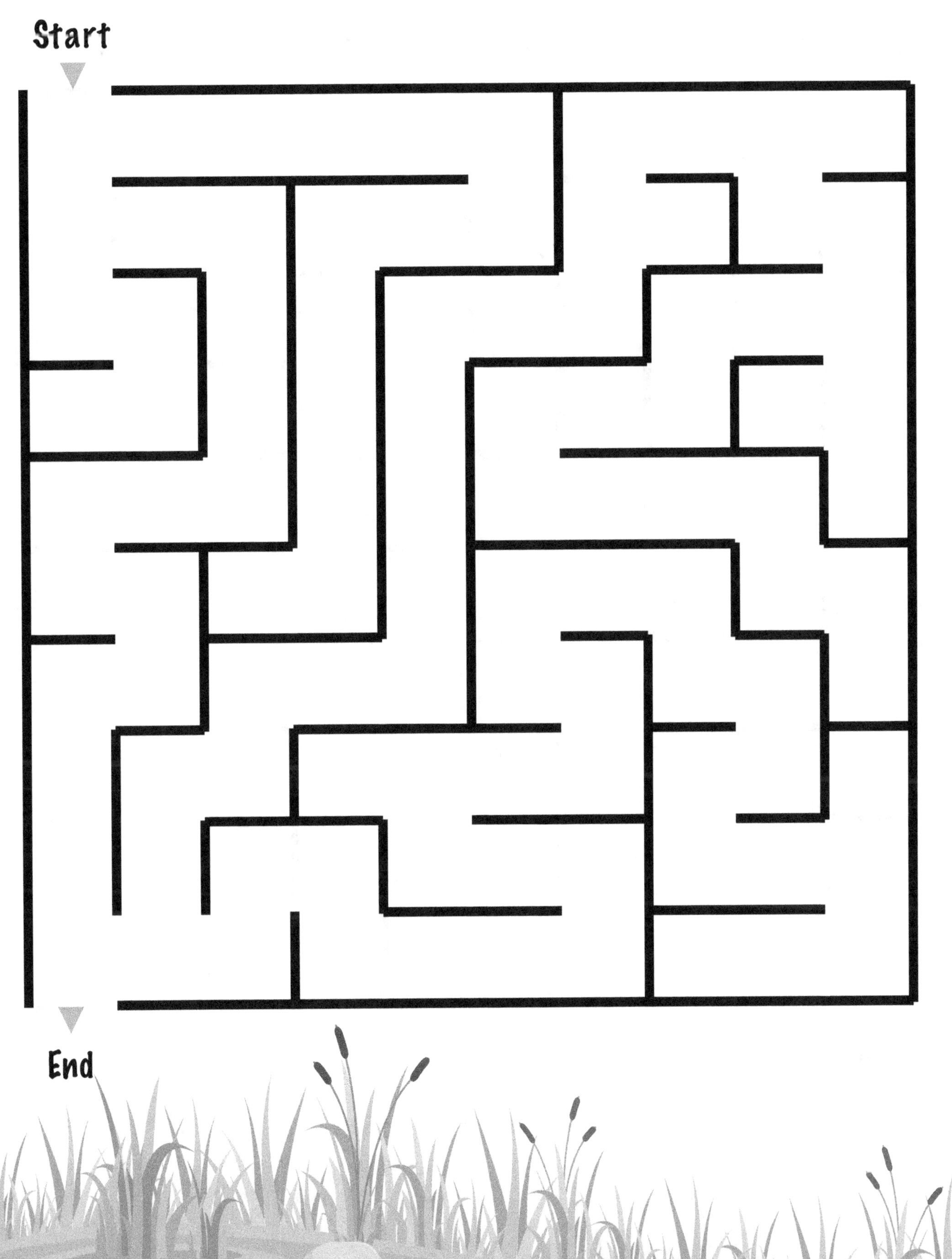

Maze 16

Maze 17

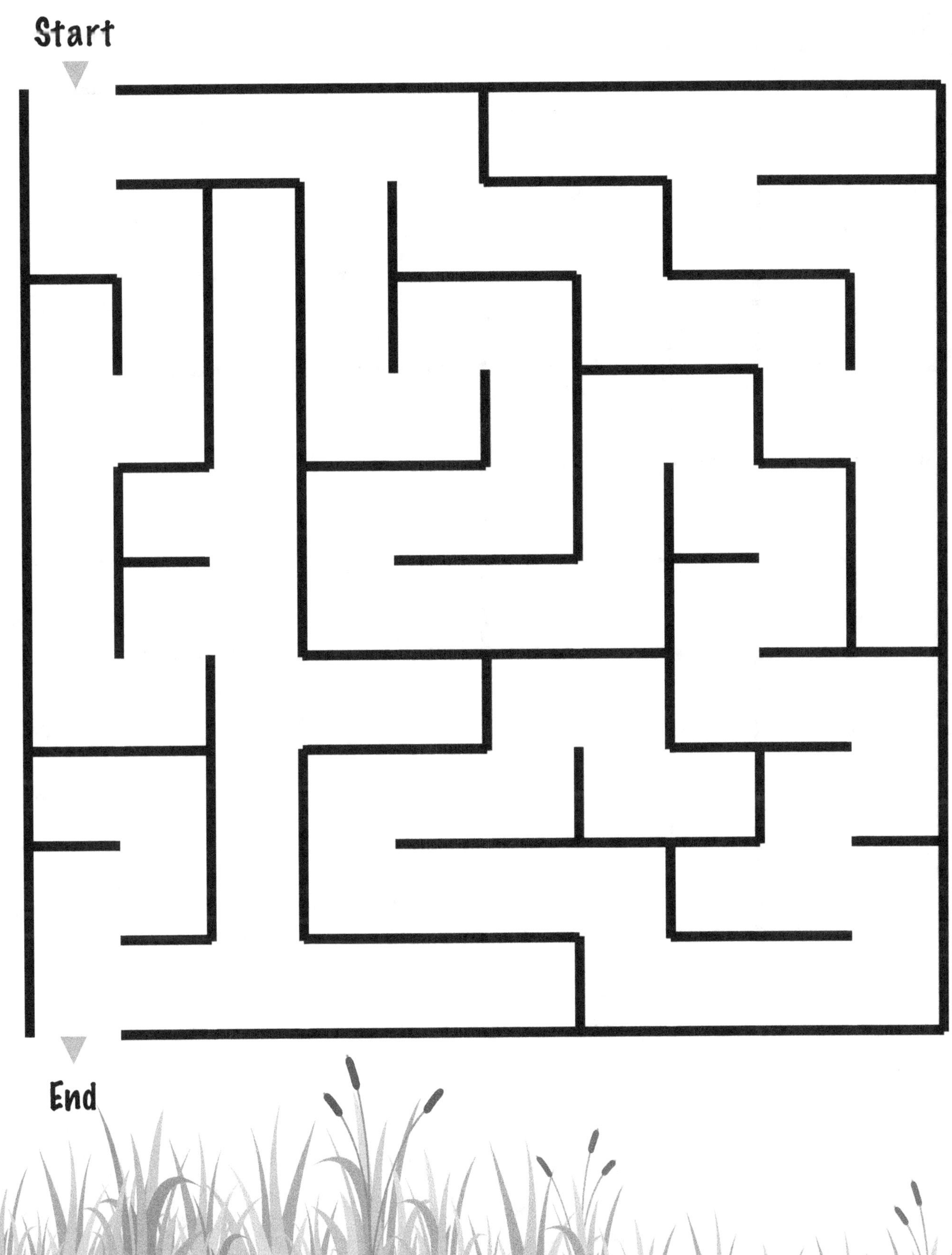

Maze 18

Maze 19

Start

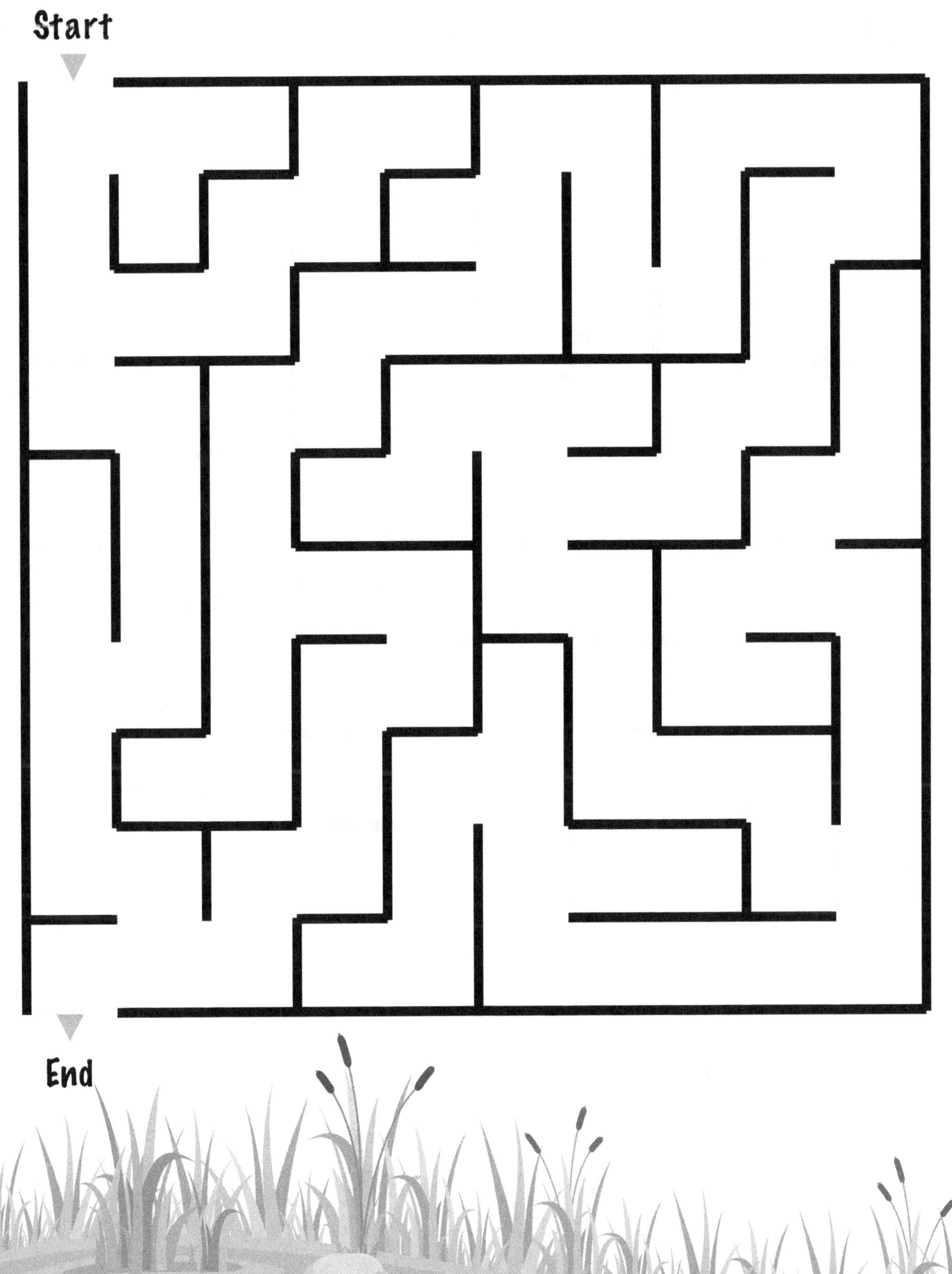

End

Maze 20

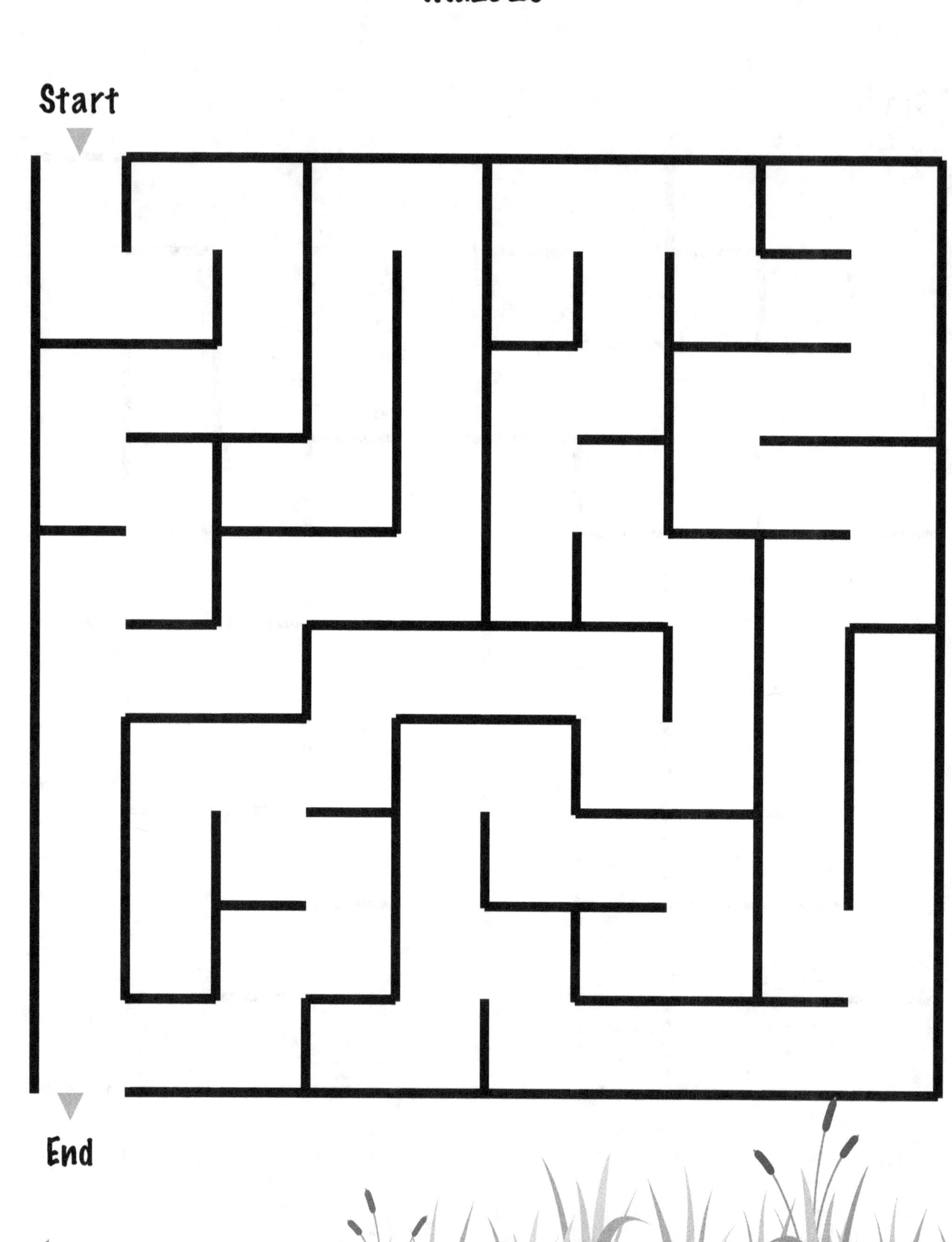

Maze 21

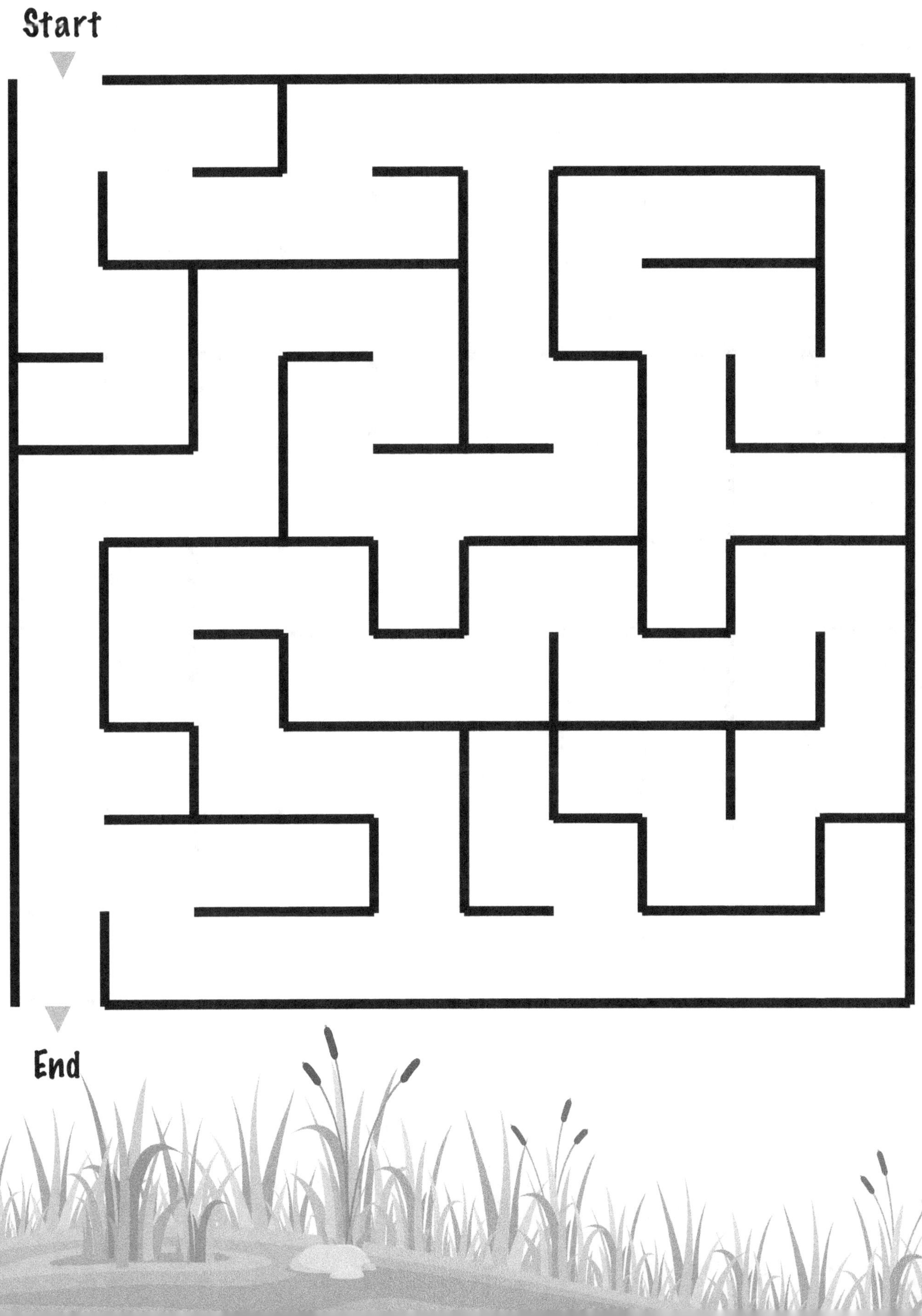

Start

End

Maze 22

Maze 23

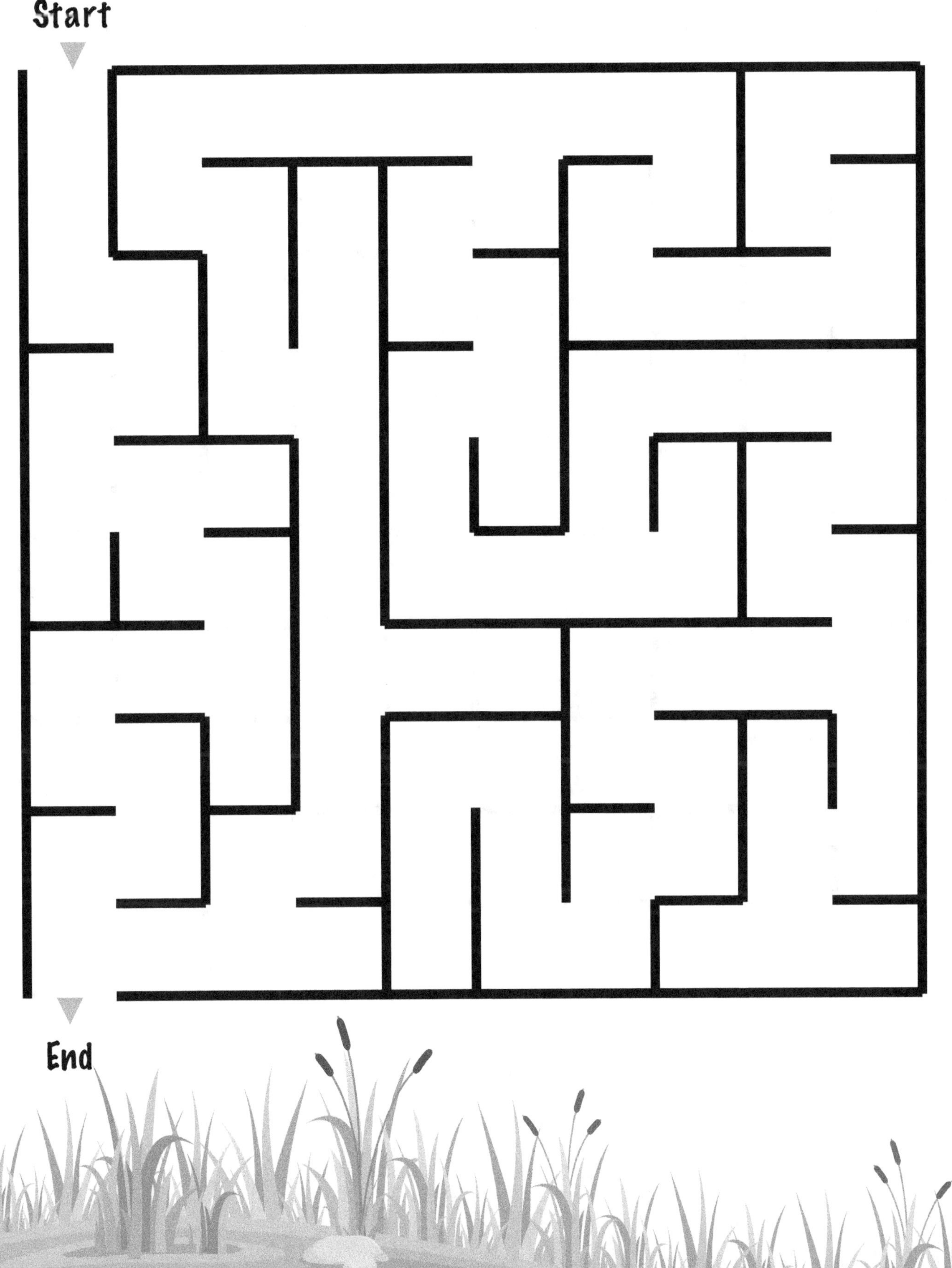

Maze 24

Start

End

Maze 25

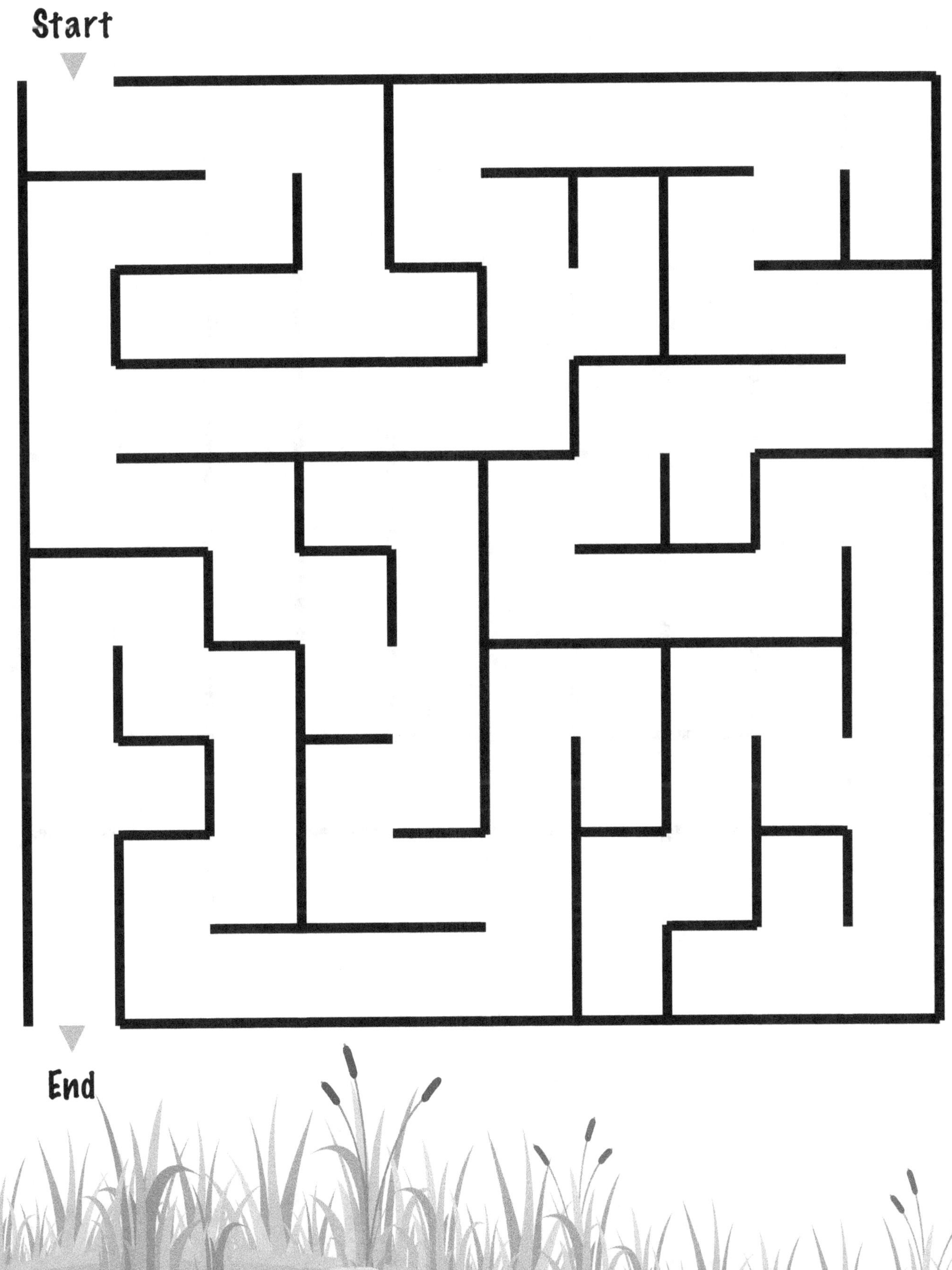

Maze 26

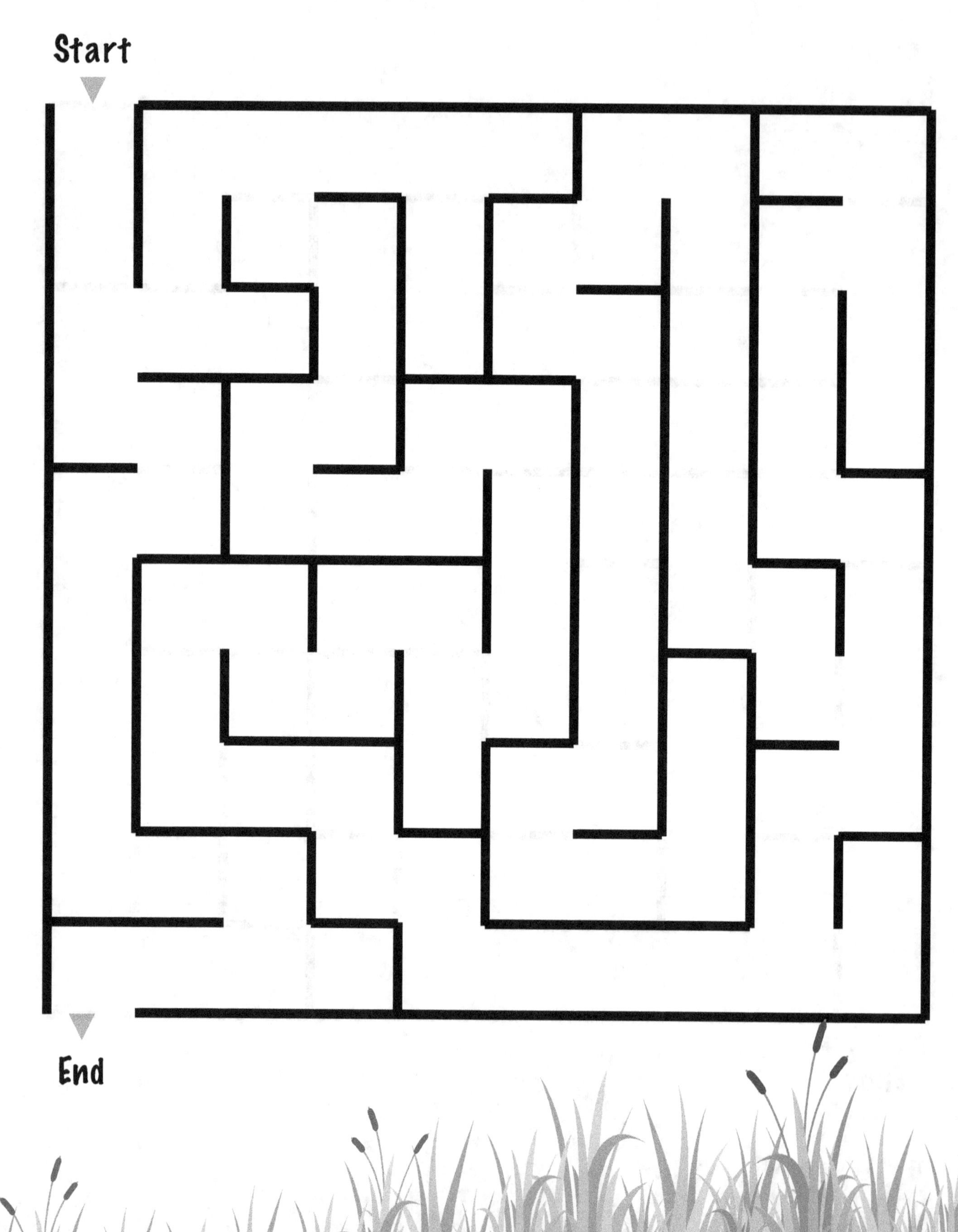

Maze 27

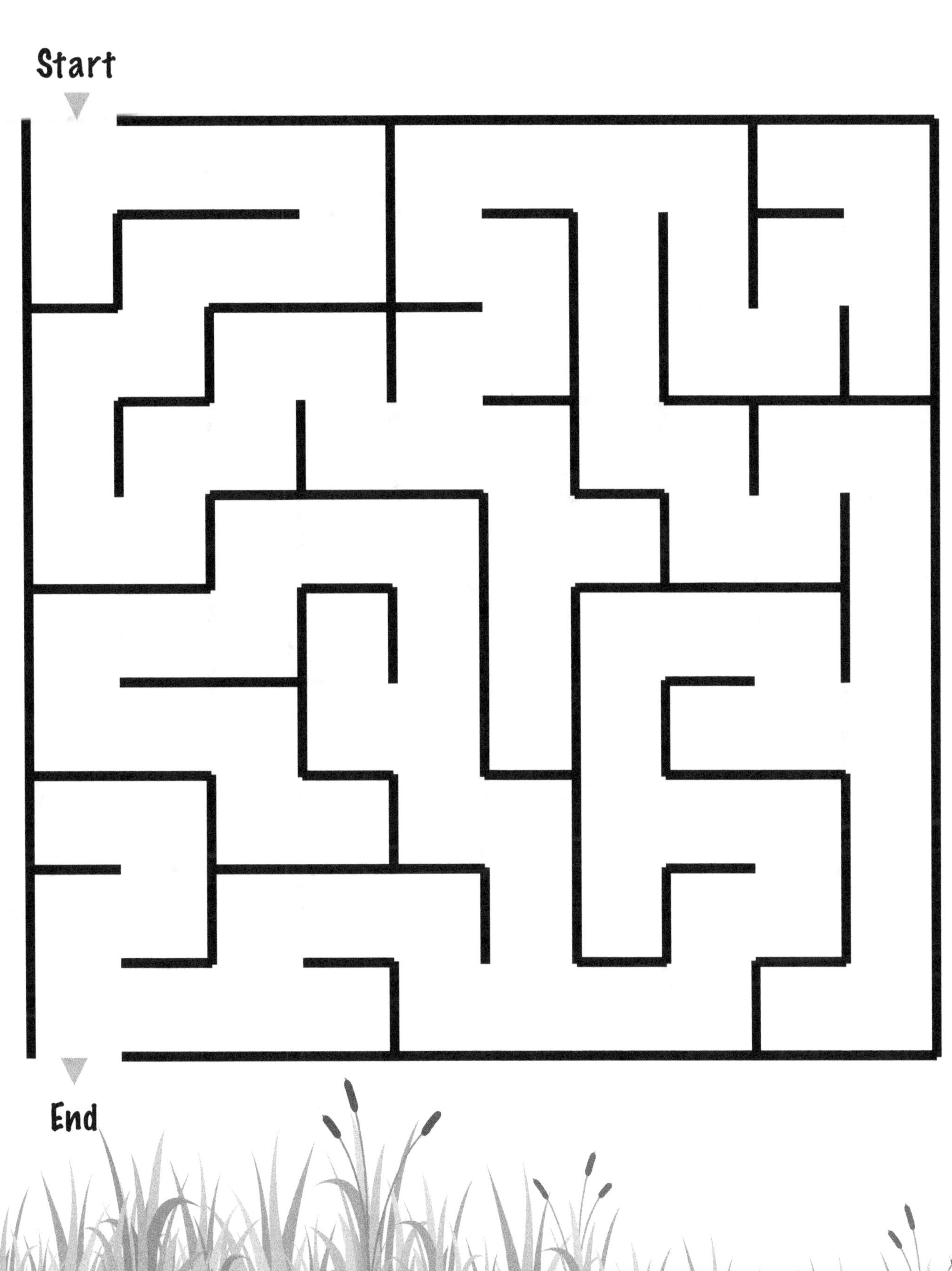

Maze 28

Maze 29

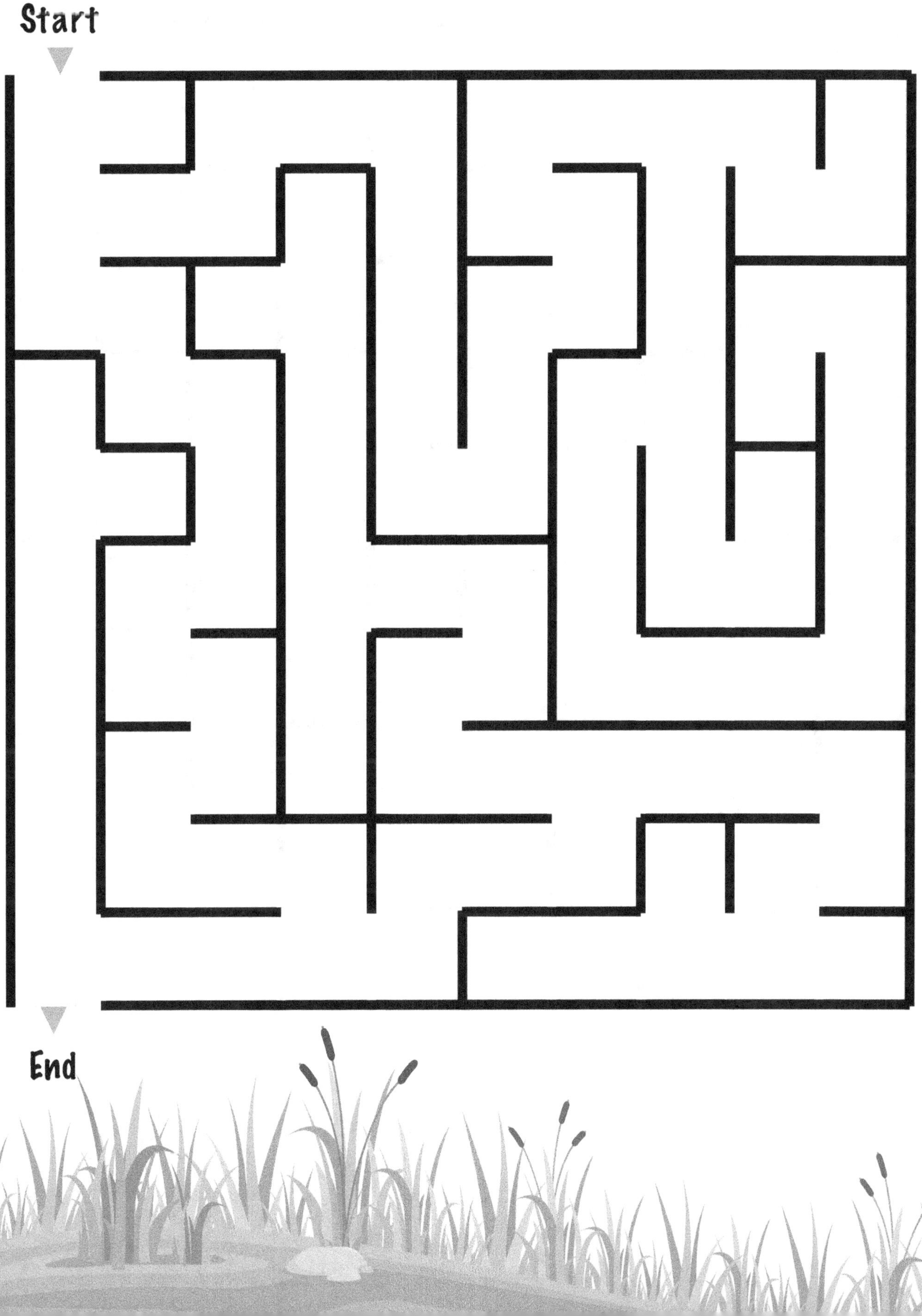

Start

End

Maze 30

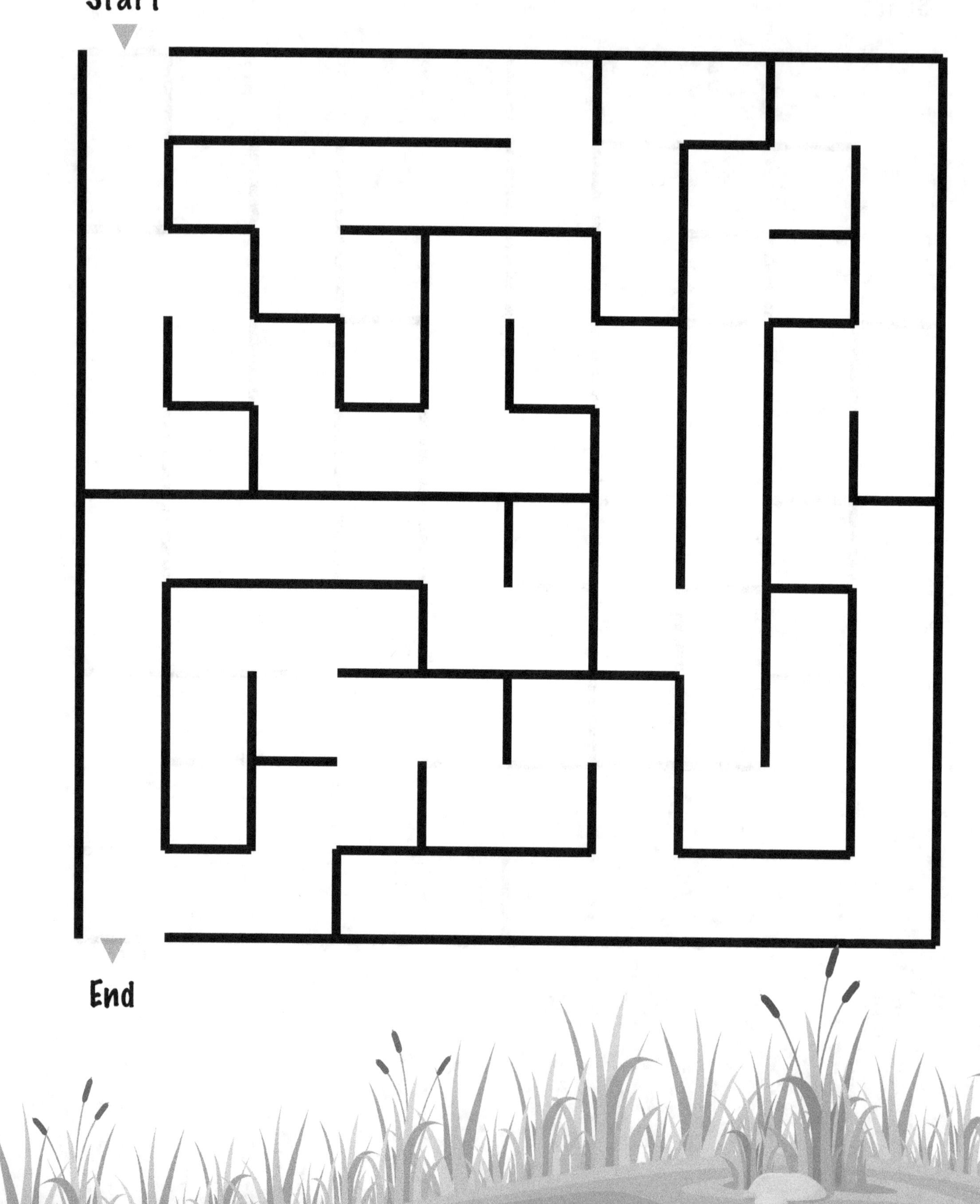

Maze 31

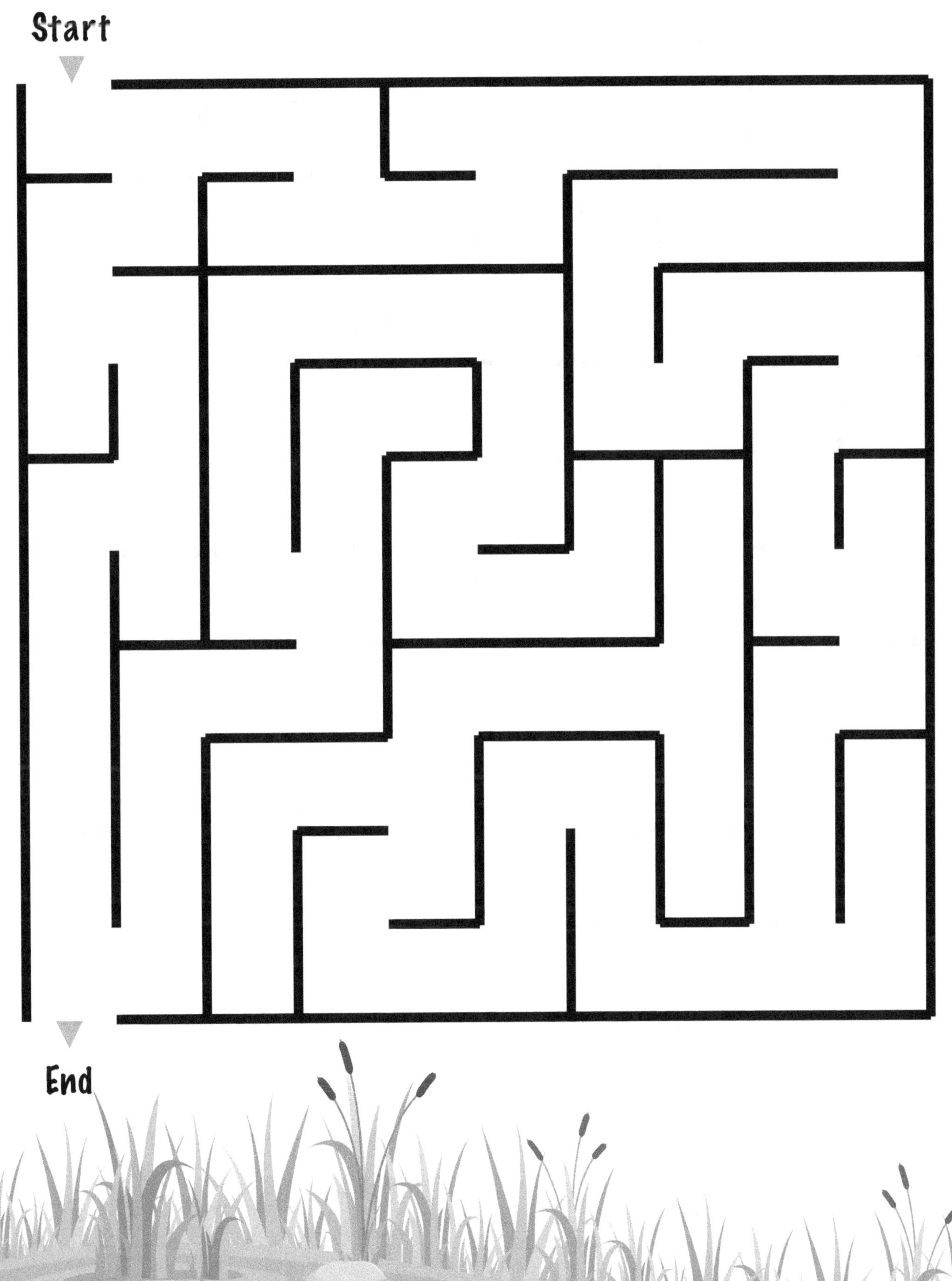

Maze 32

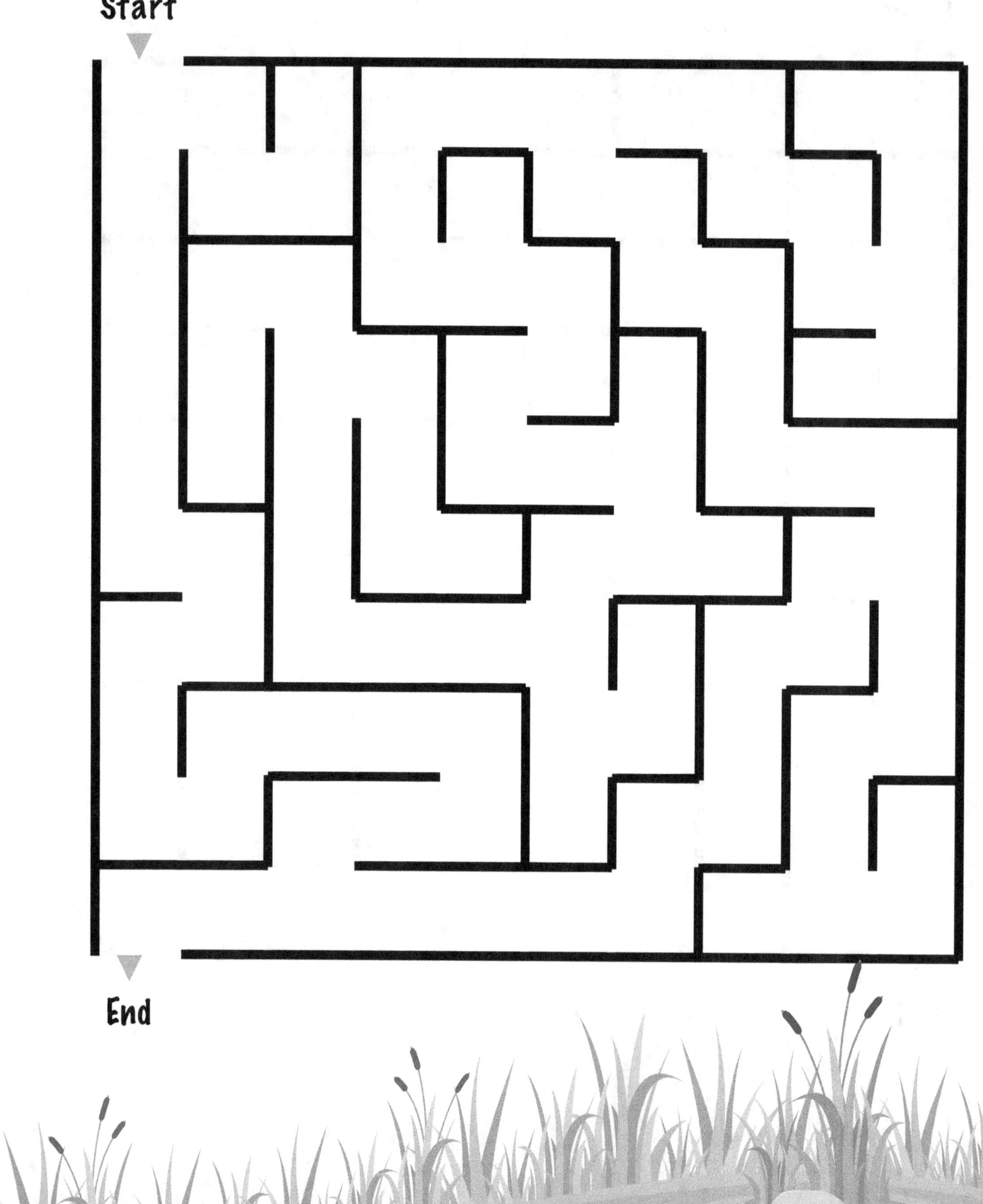

Maze 33

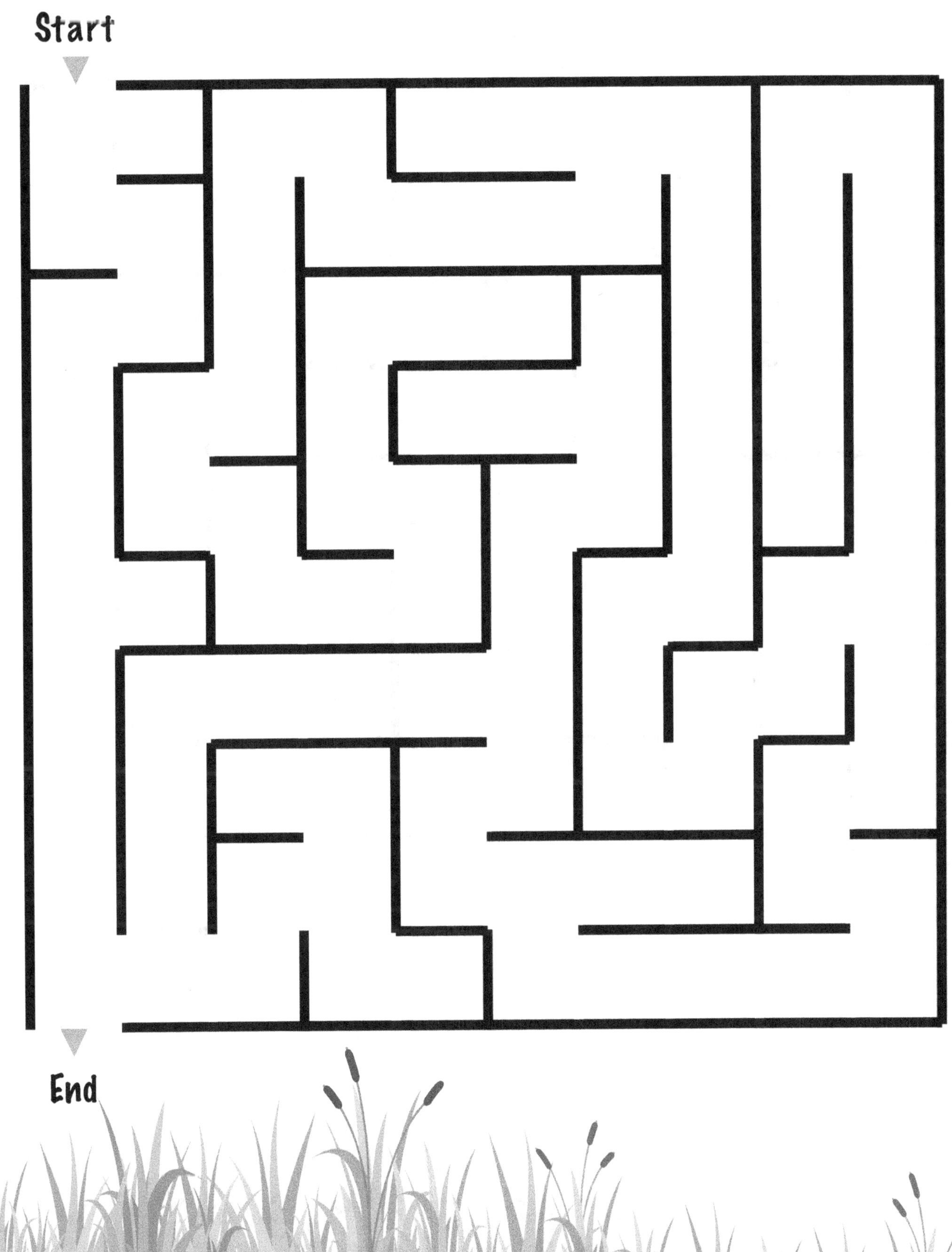

Maze 34

Maze 35

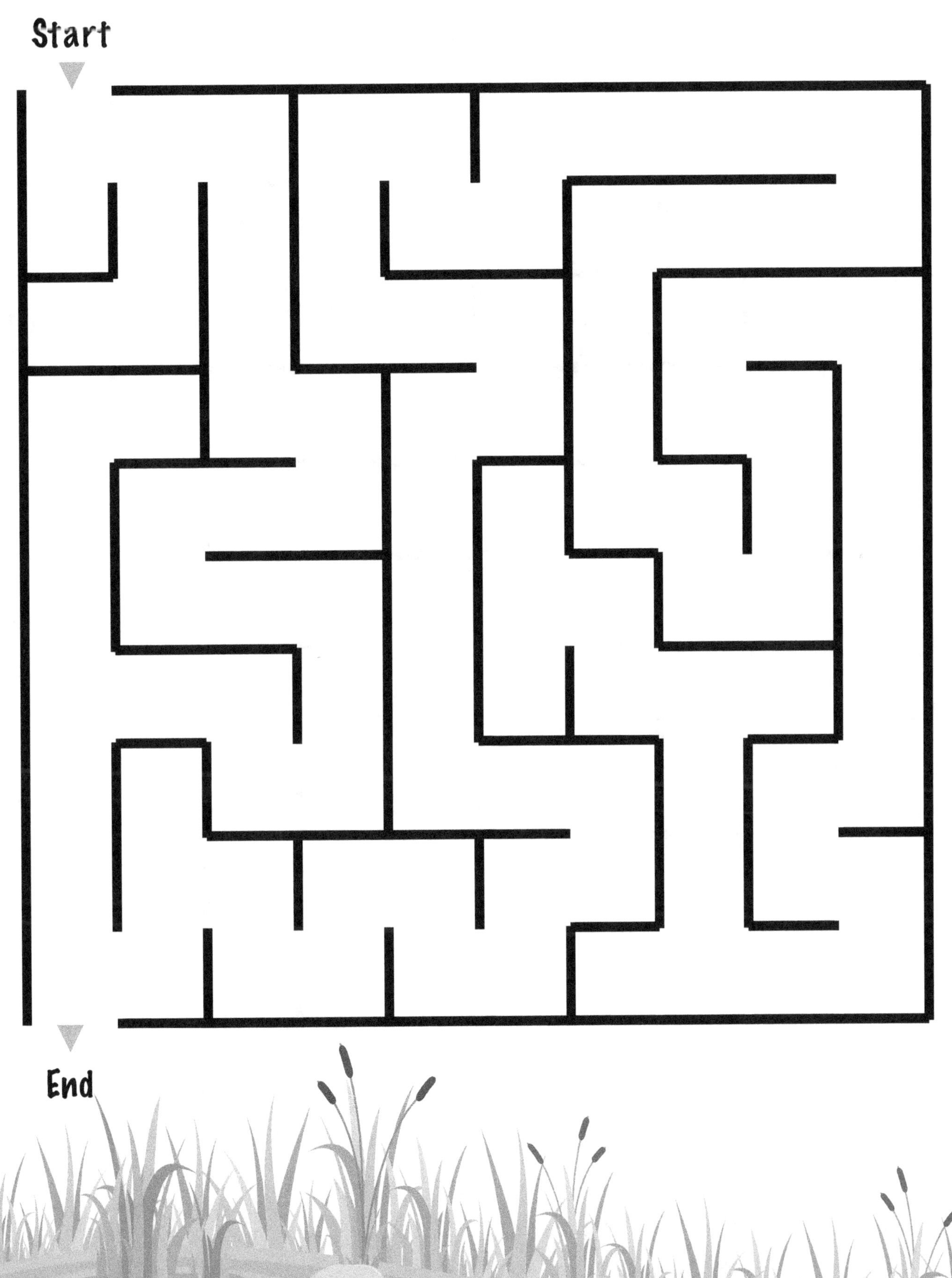

Maze 36

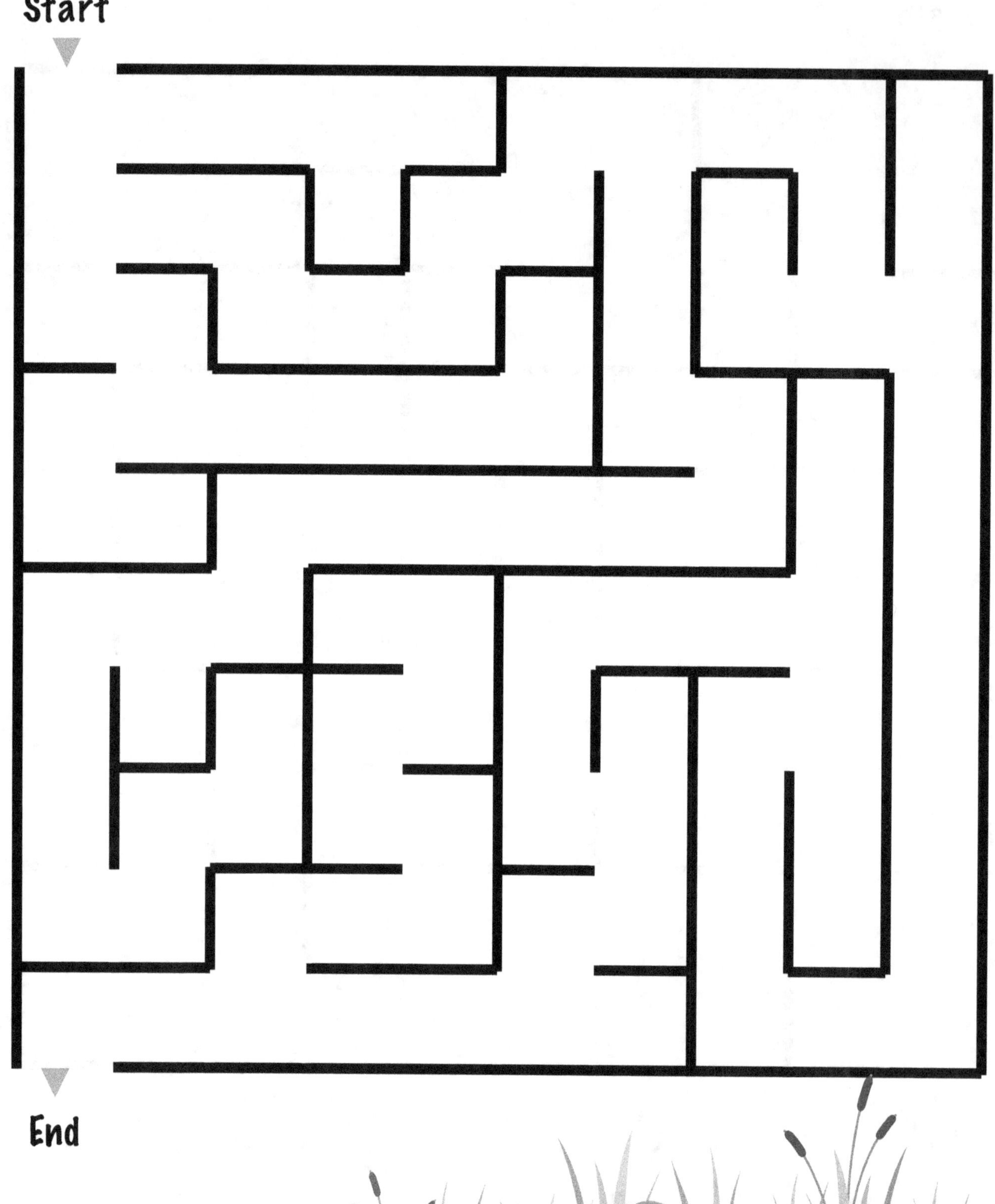

Maze 37

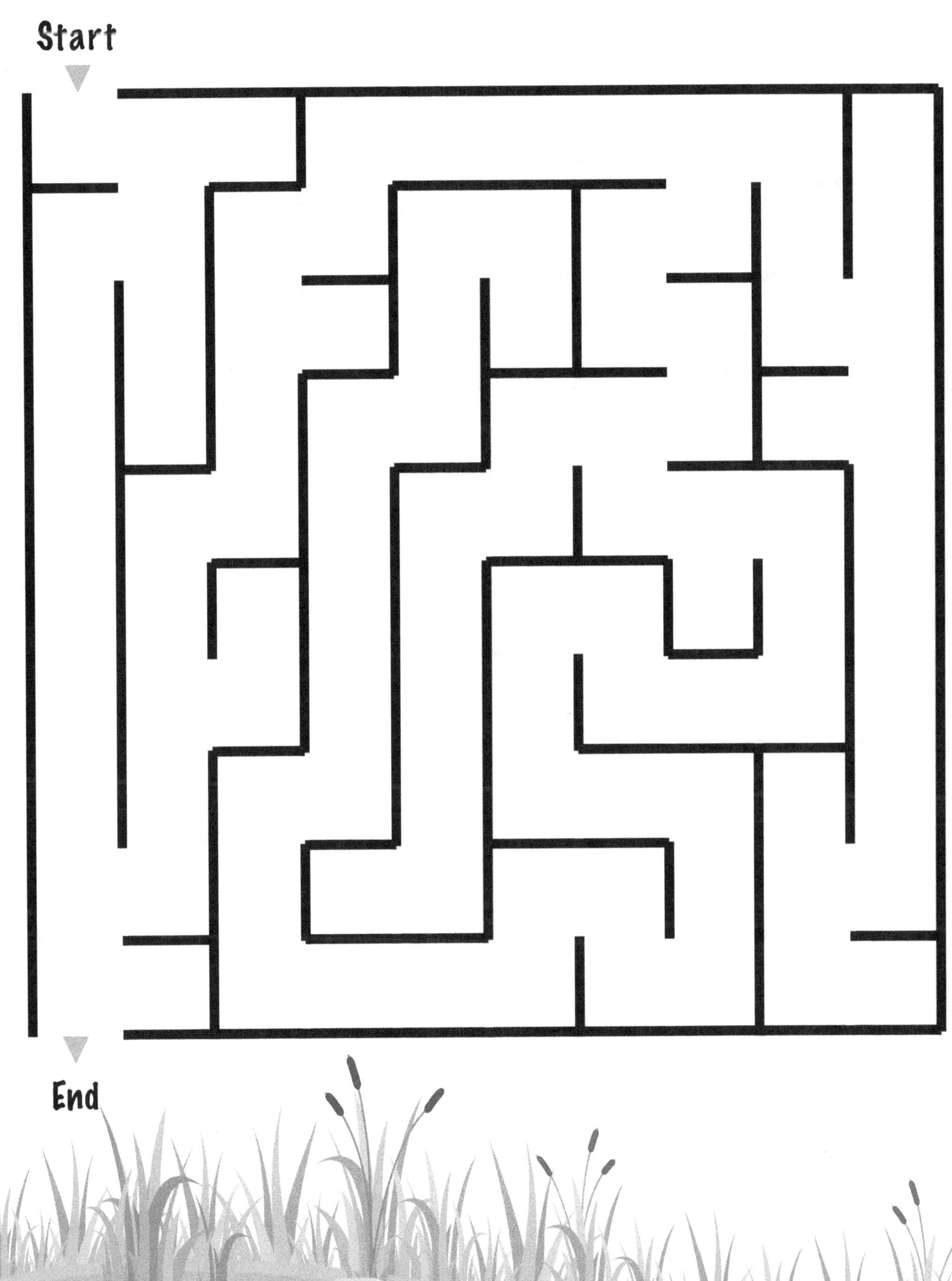

Start

End

Maze 39

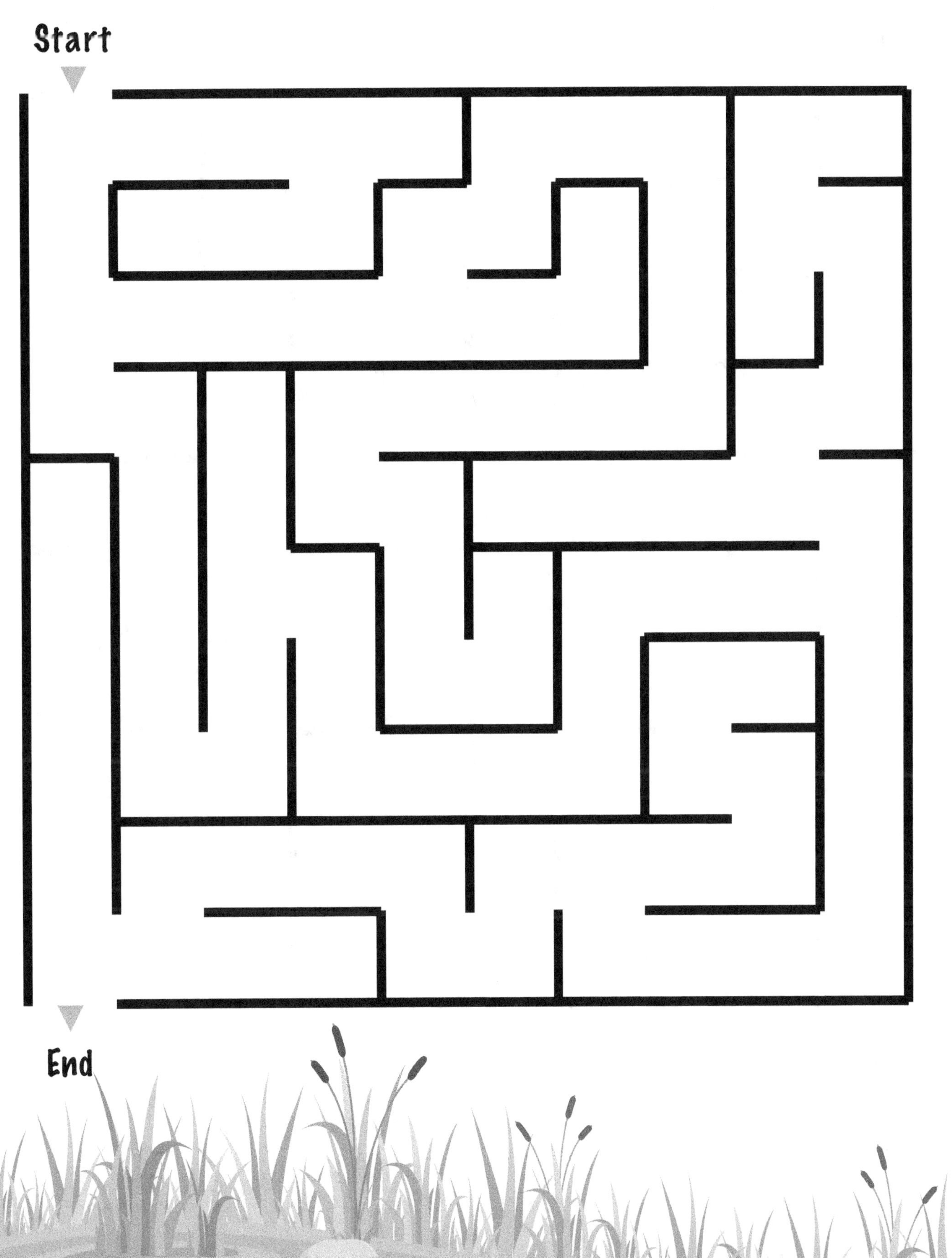

Maze 40

Maze 41

Start

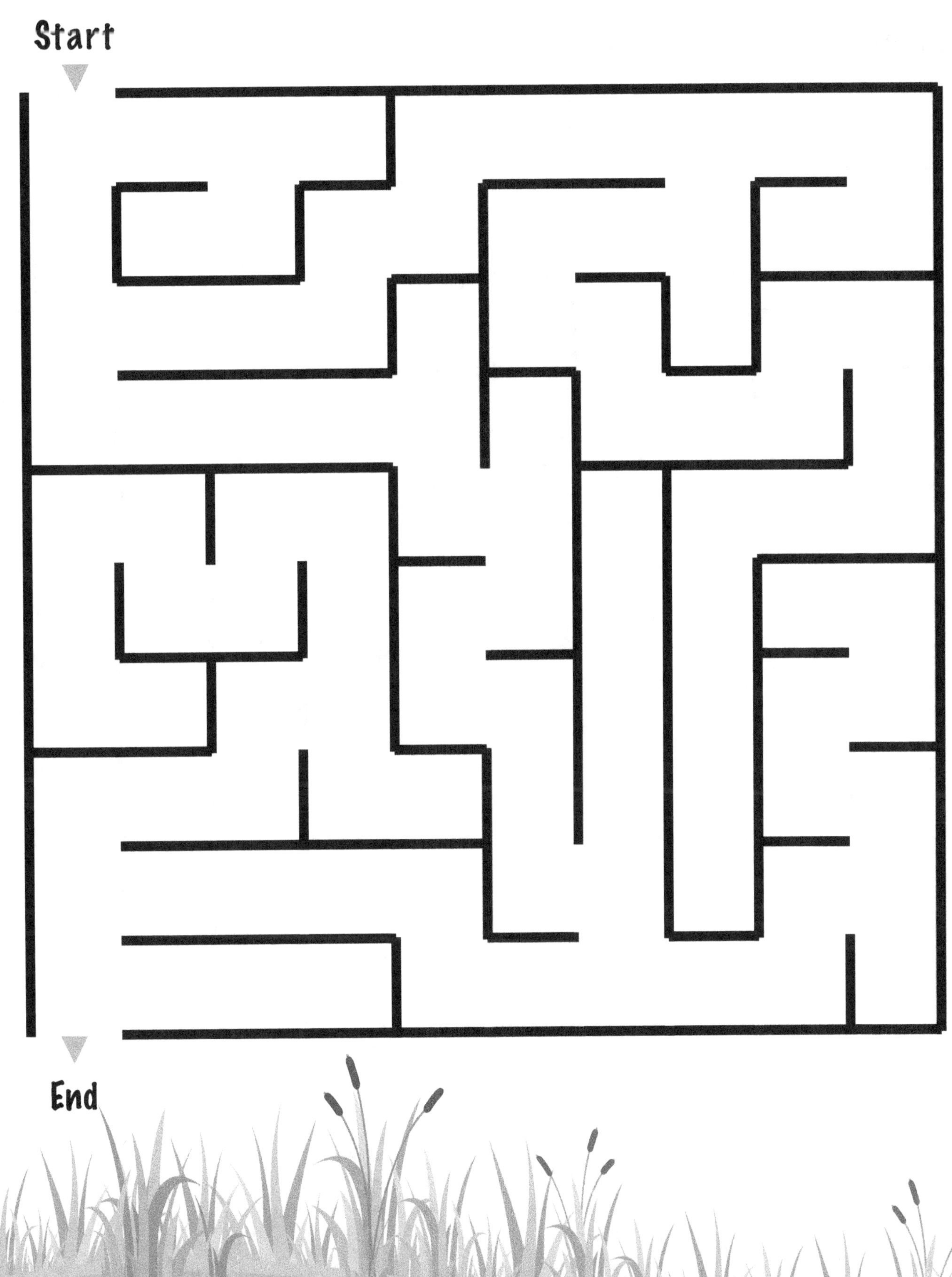

End

Maze 42

Maze 43

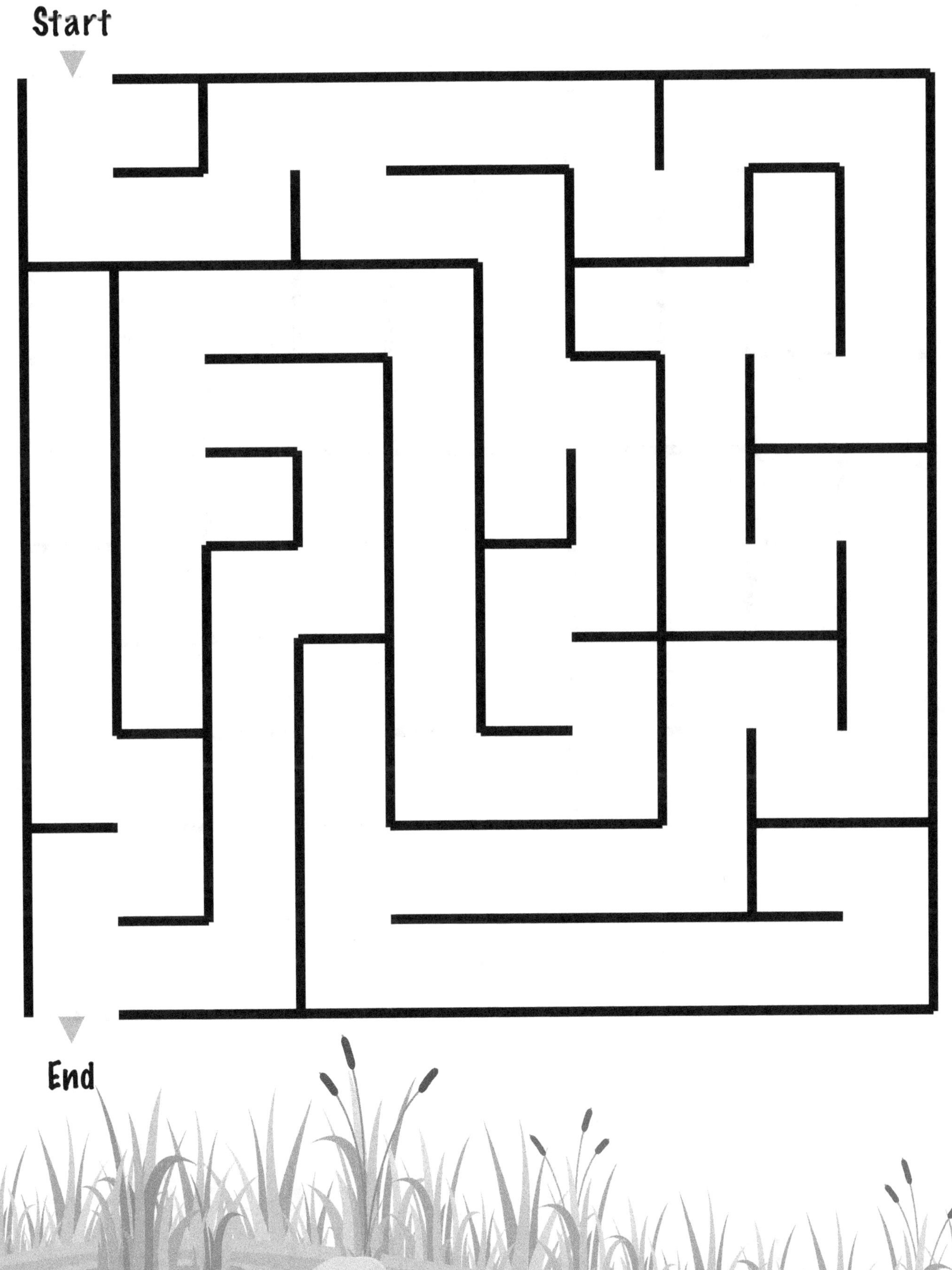

Maze 44

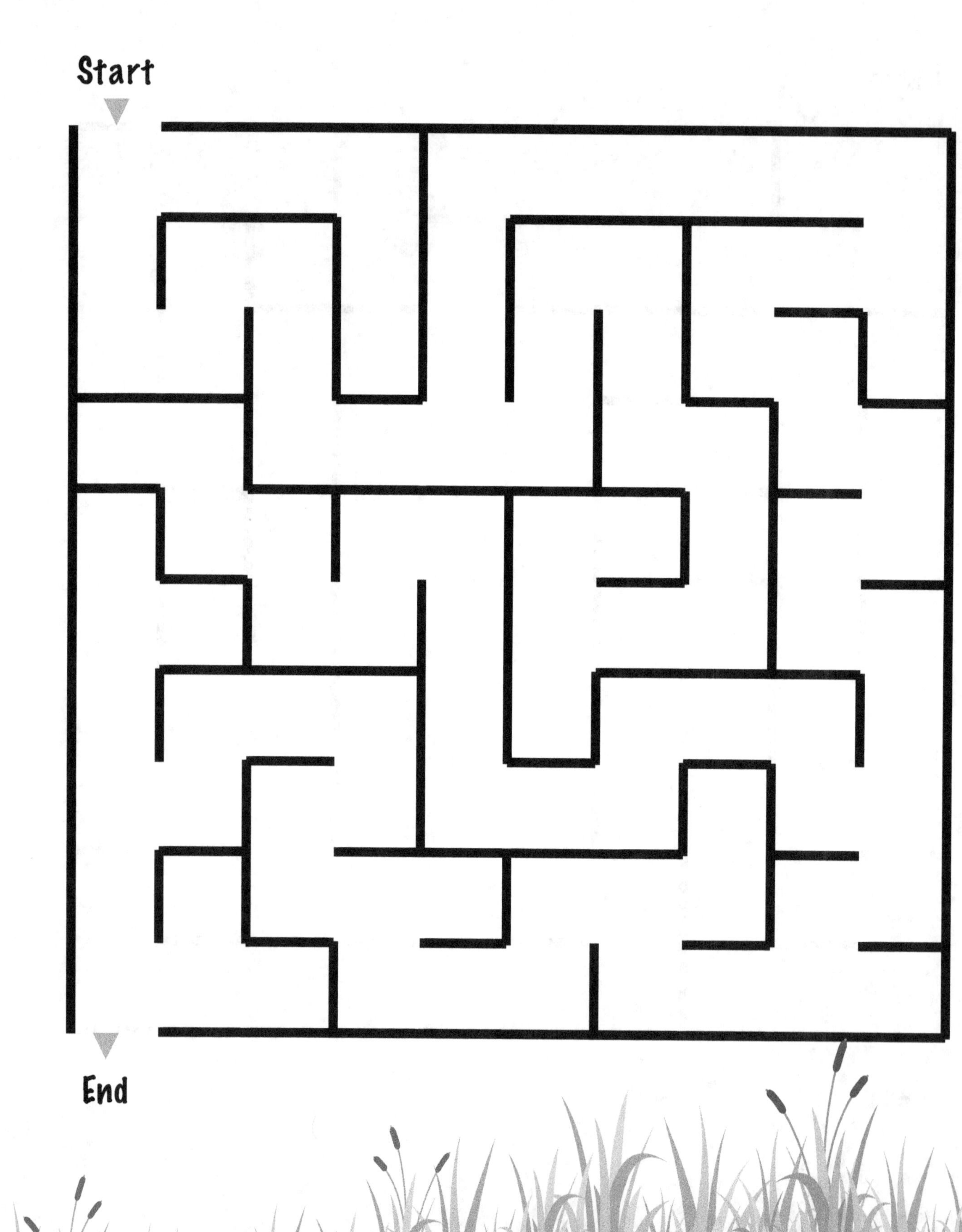

Maze 45

Start

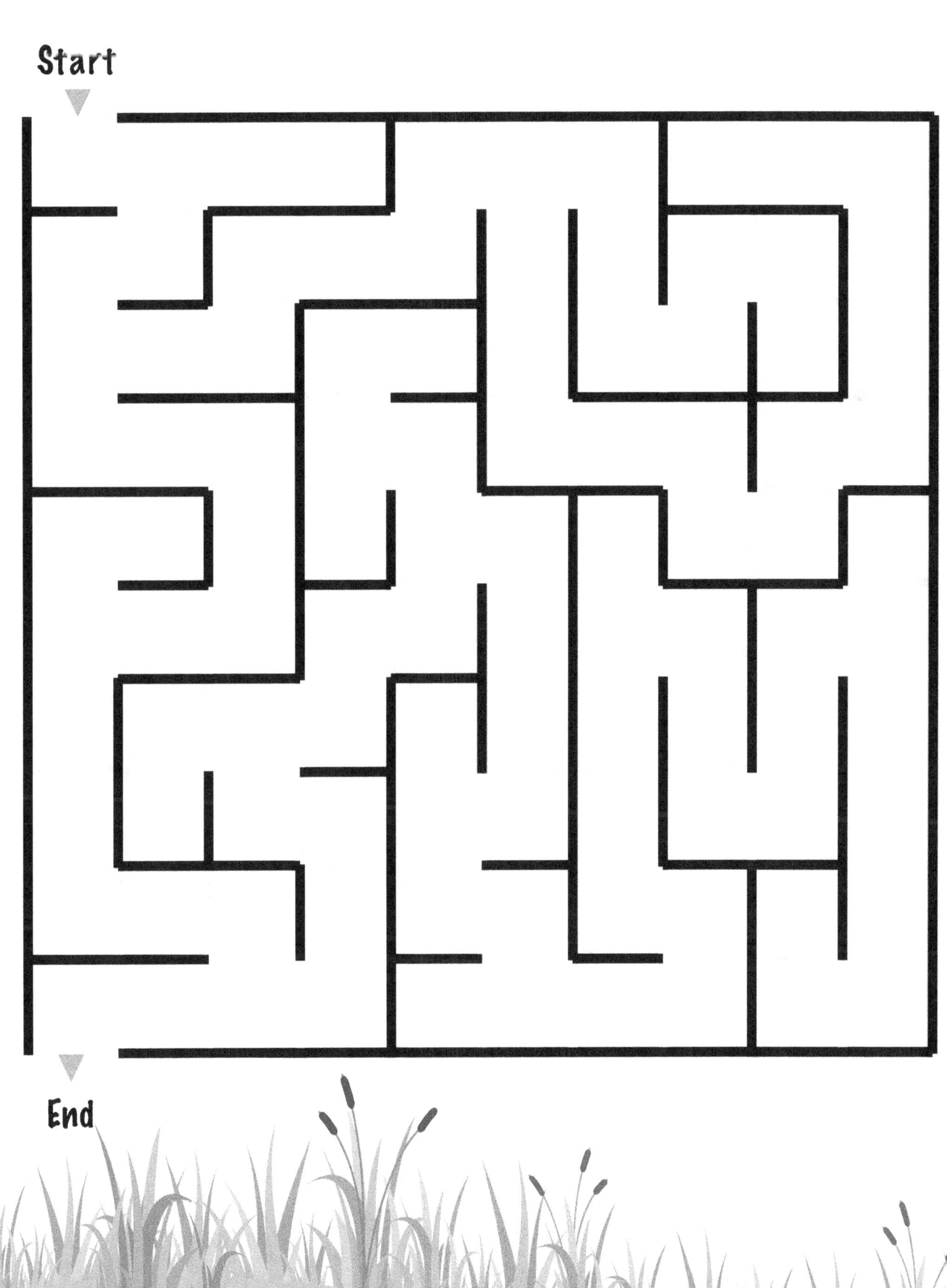

End

Maze 46

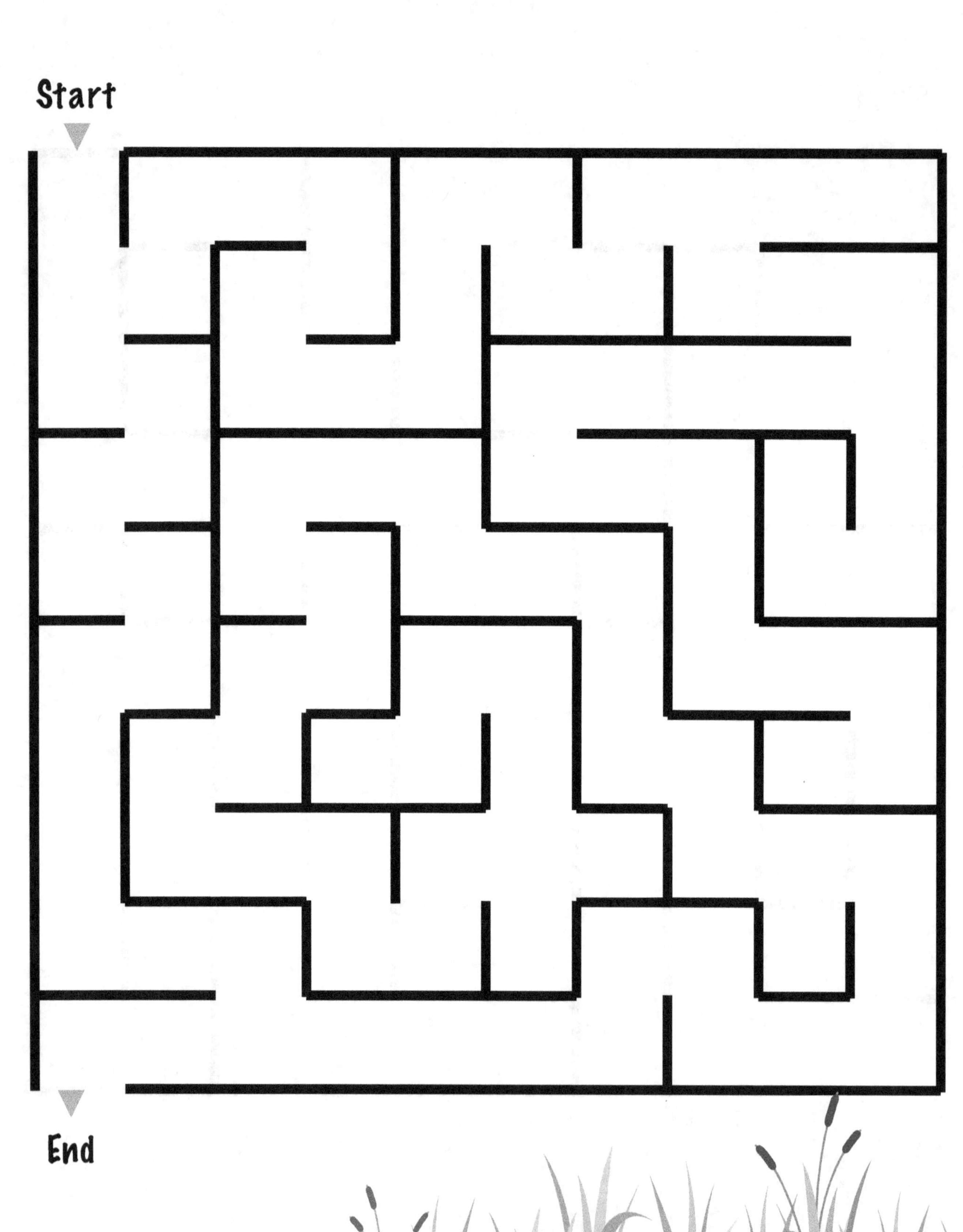

Maze 47

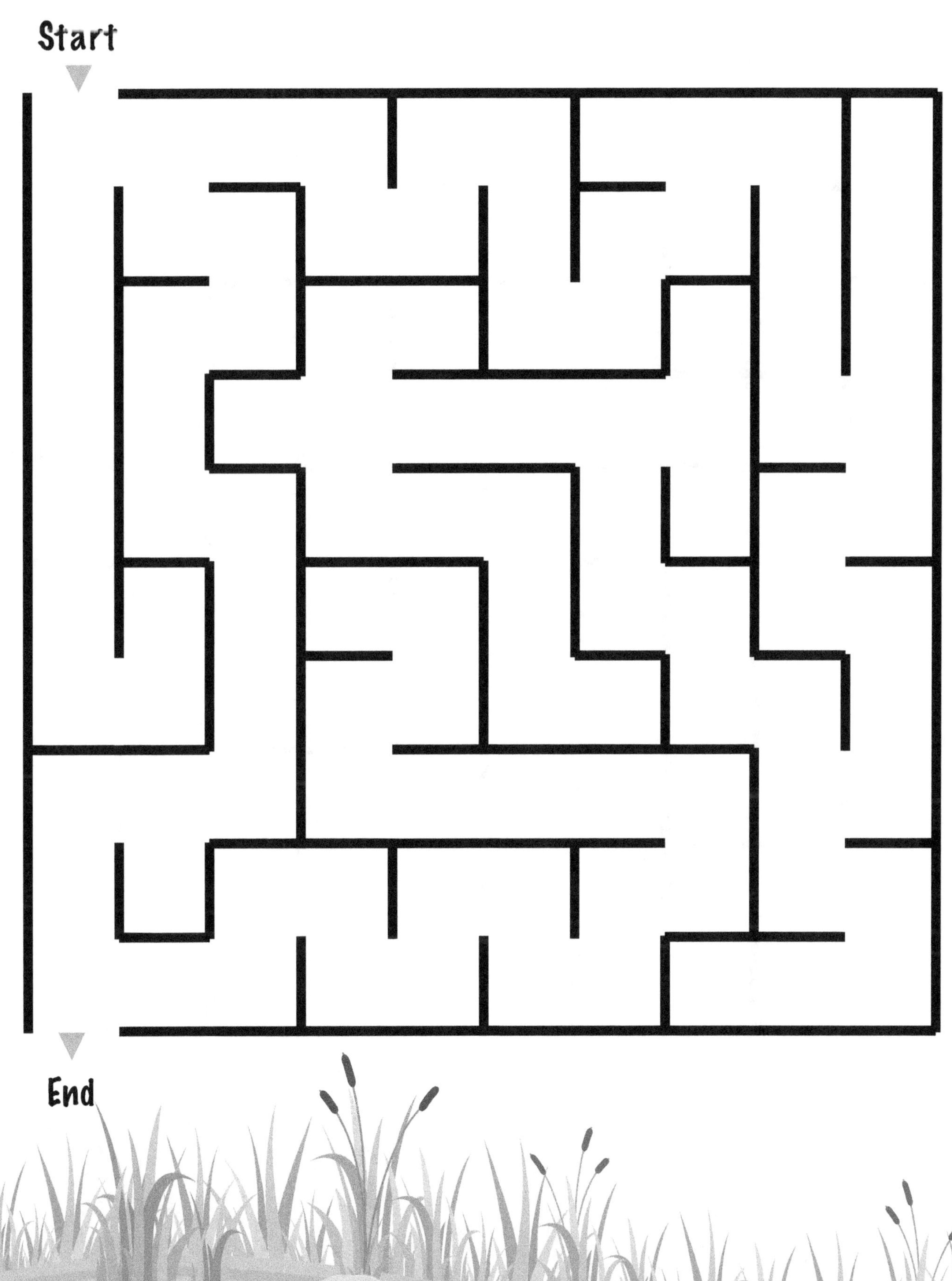

Maze 48

Maze 49

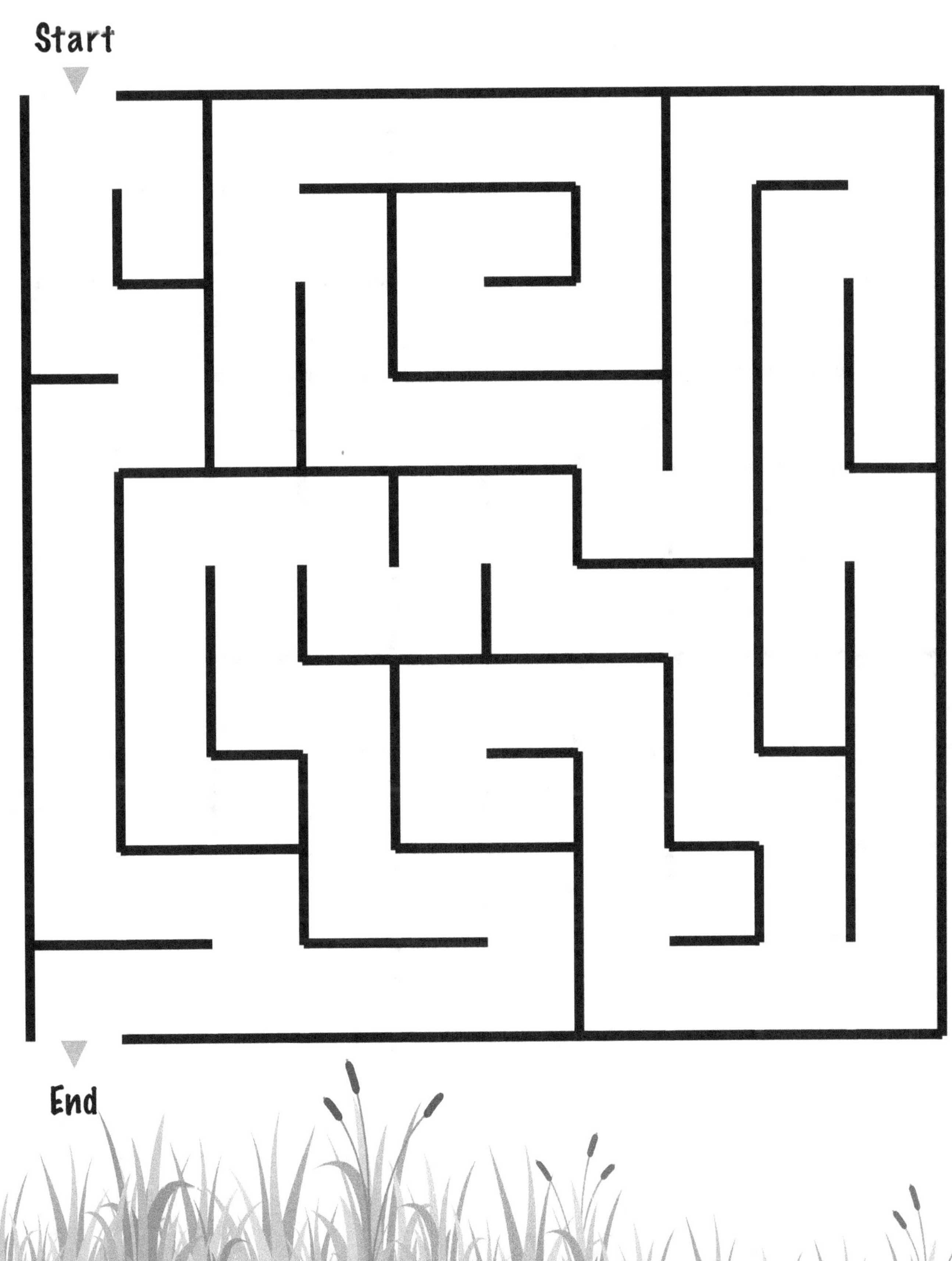

Maze 50

Maze 51

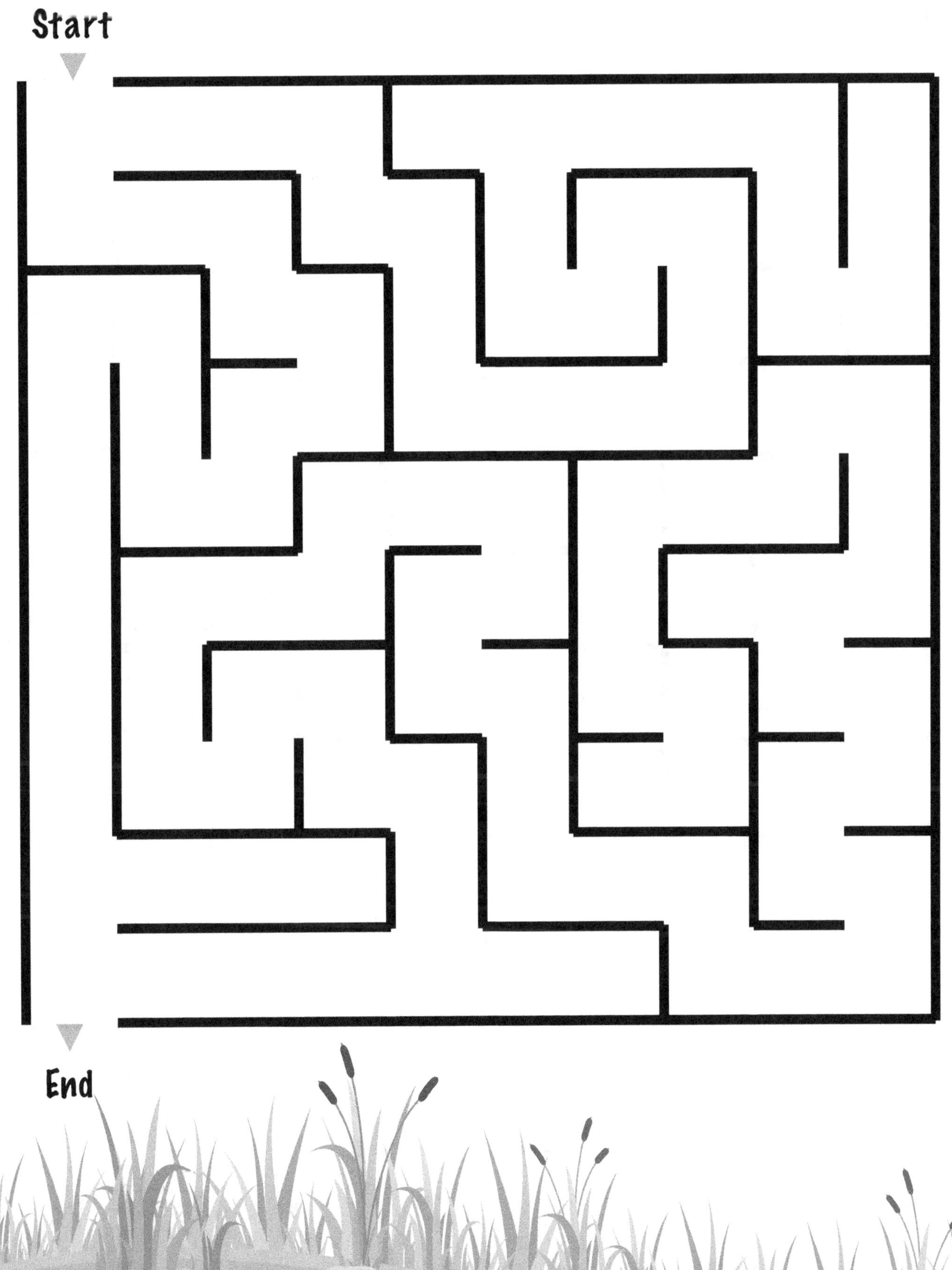

Maze 52

Maze 53

Start

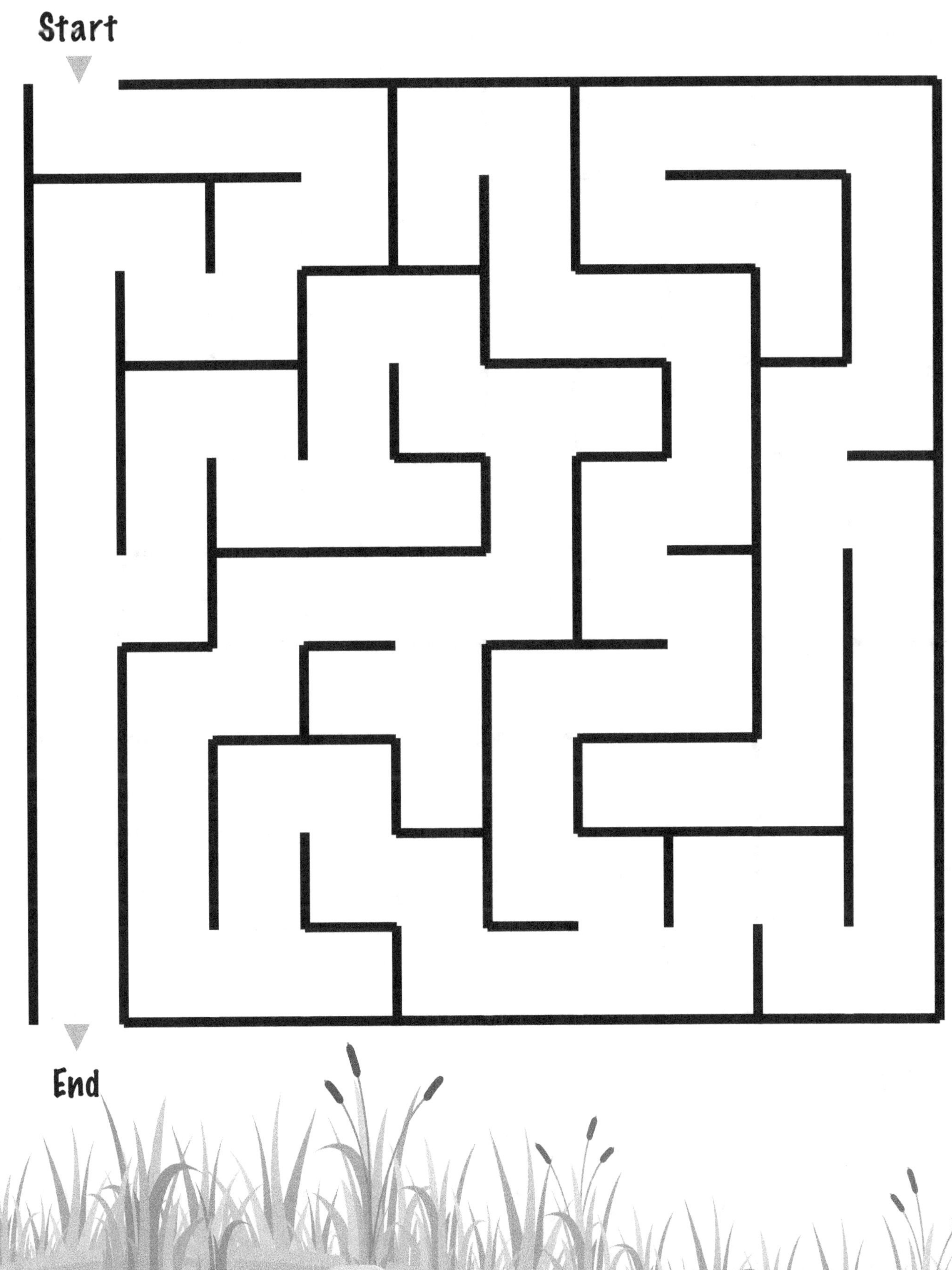

End

Maze 54

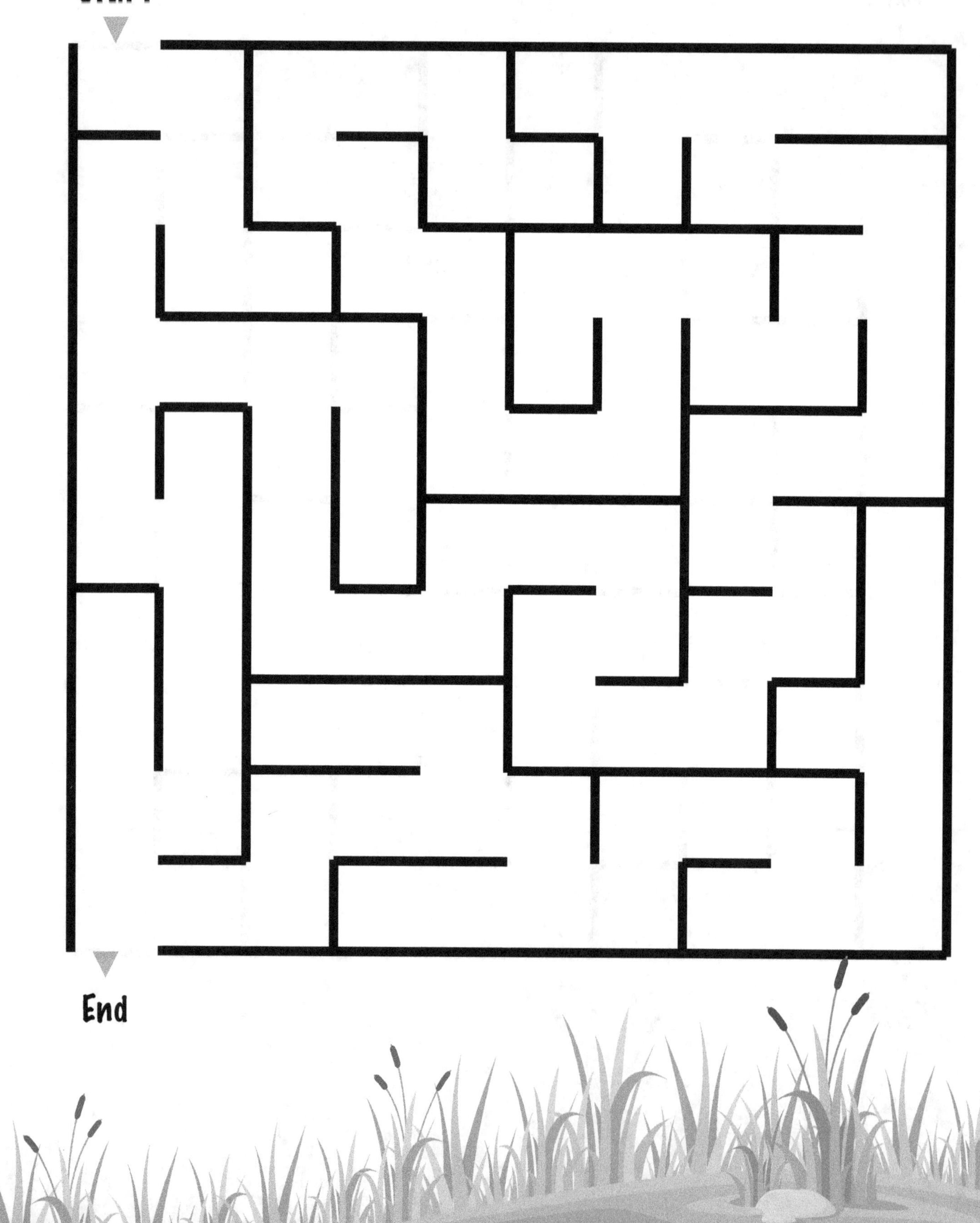

Maze 55

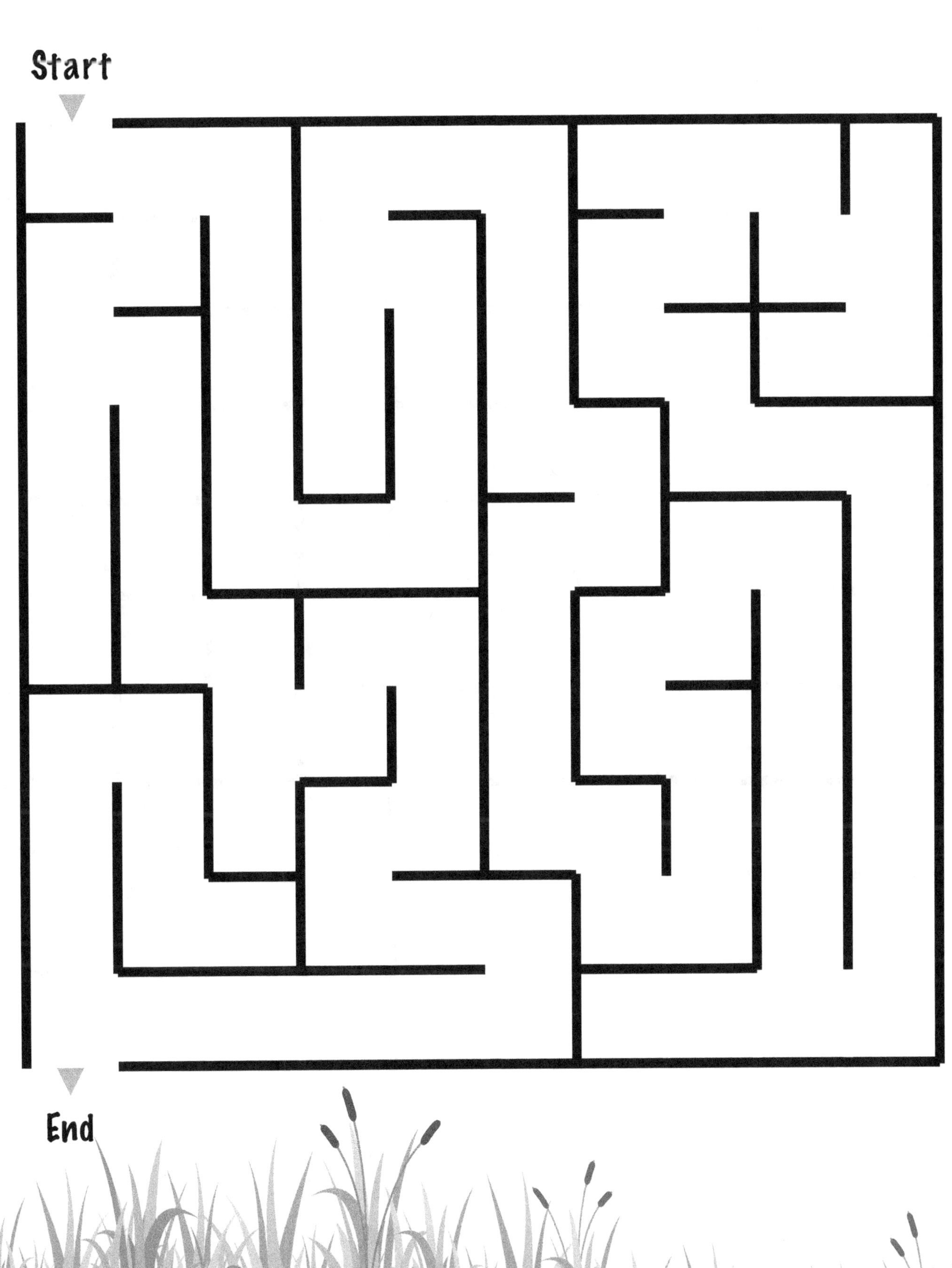

Maze 56

Start

End

Maze 57

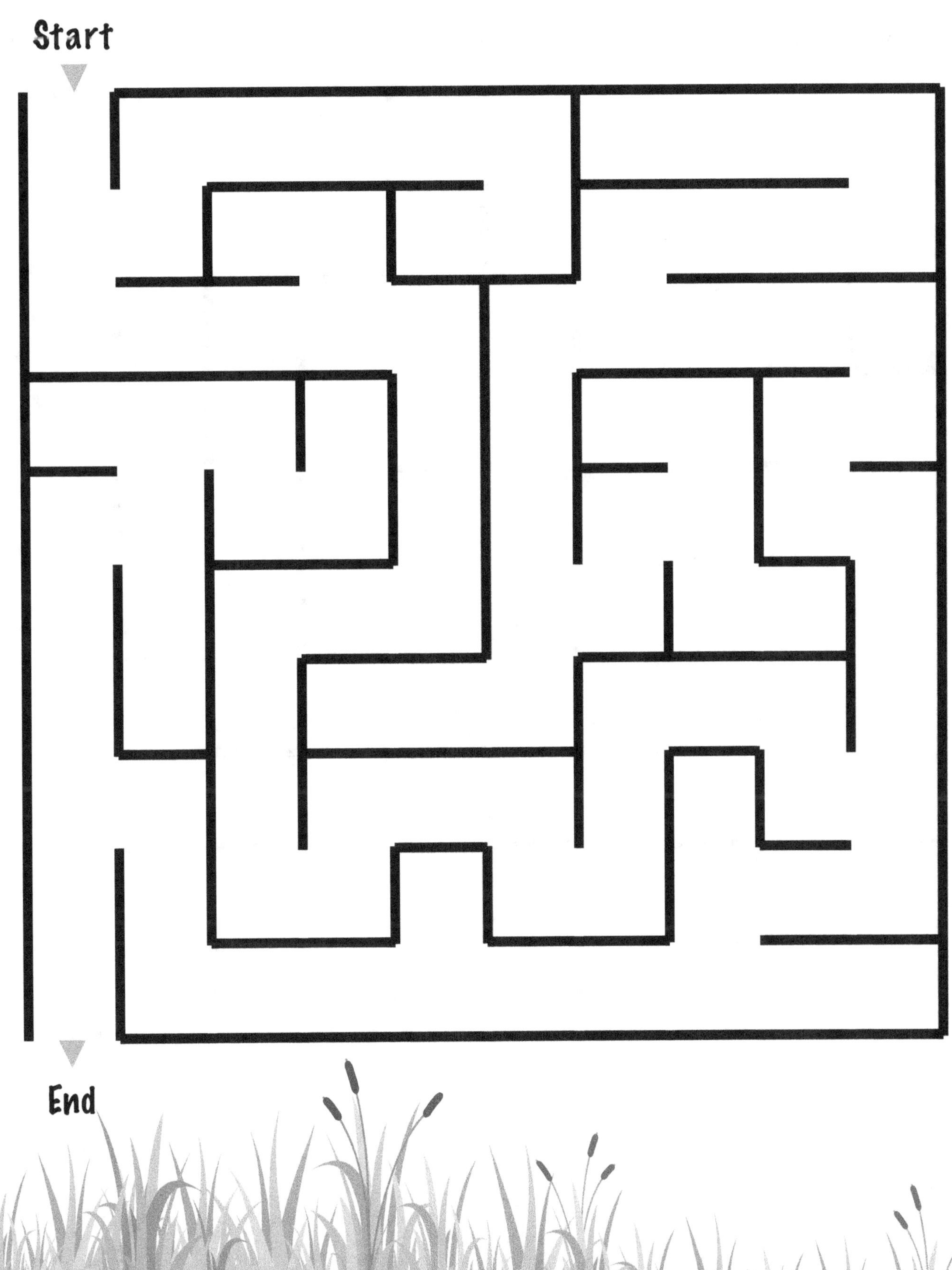

Maze 58

Maze 59

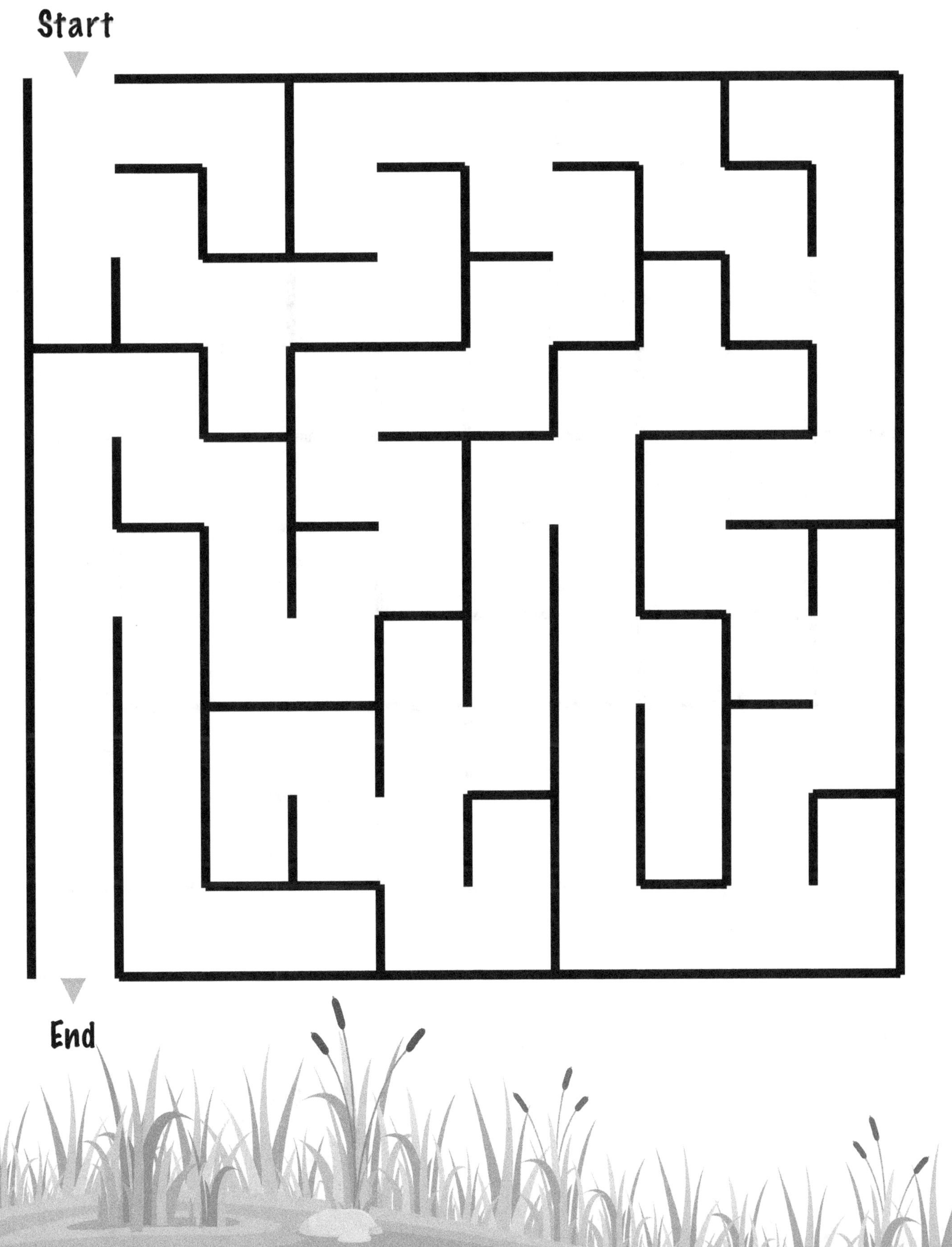

Maze 60

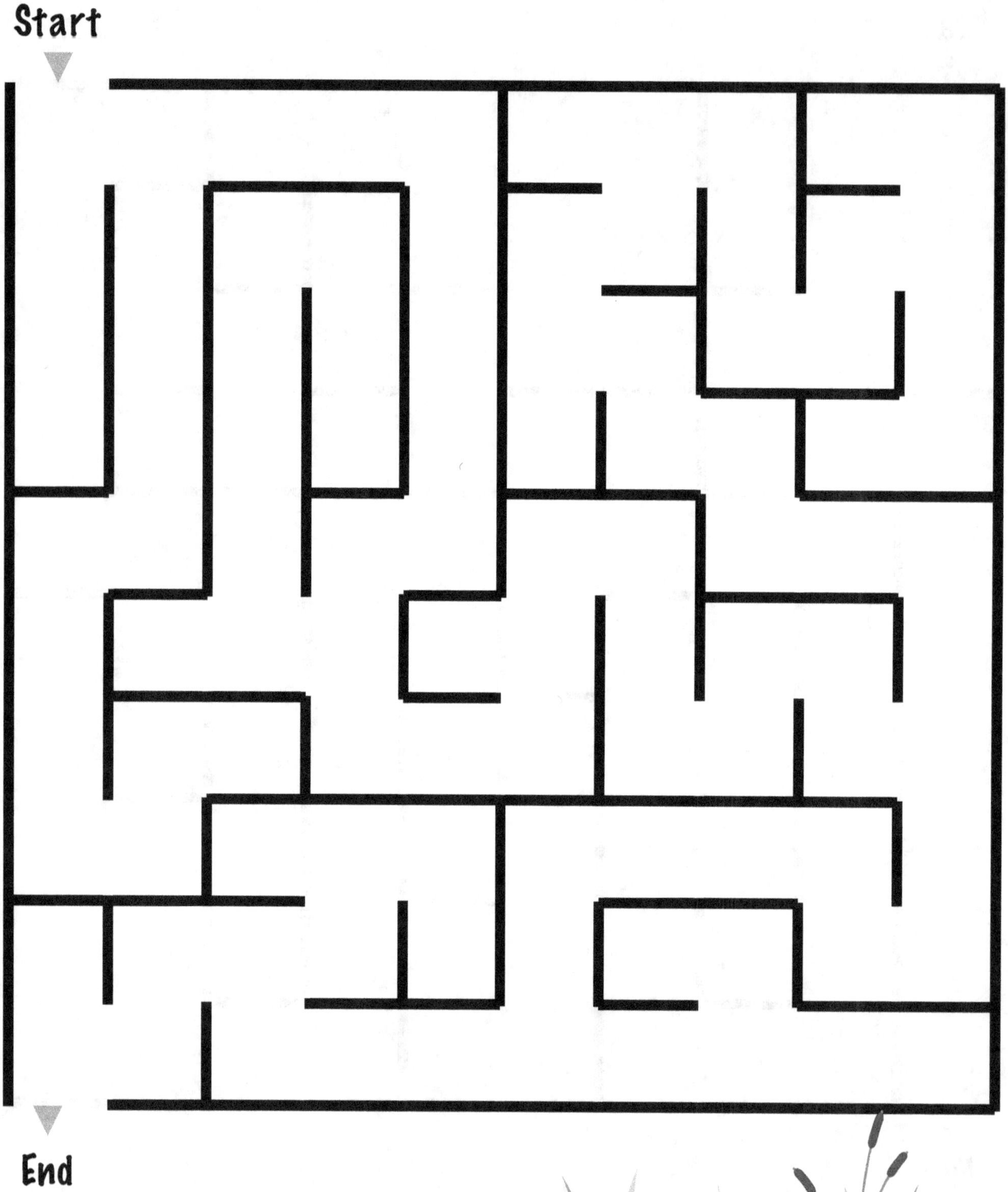

Maze 61

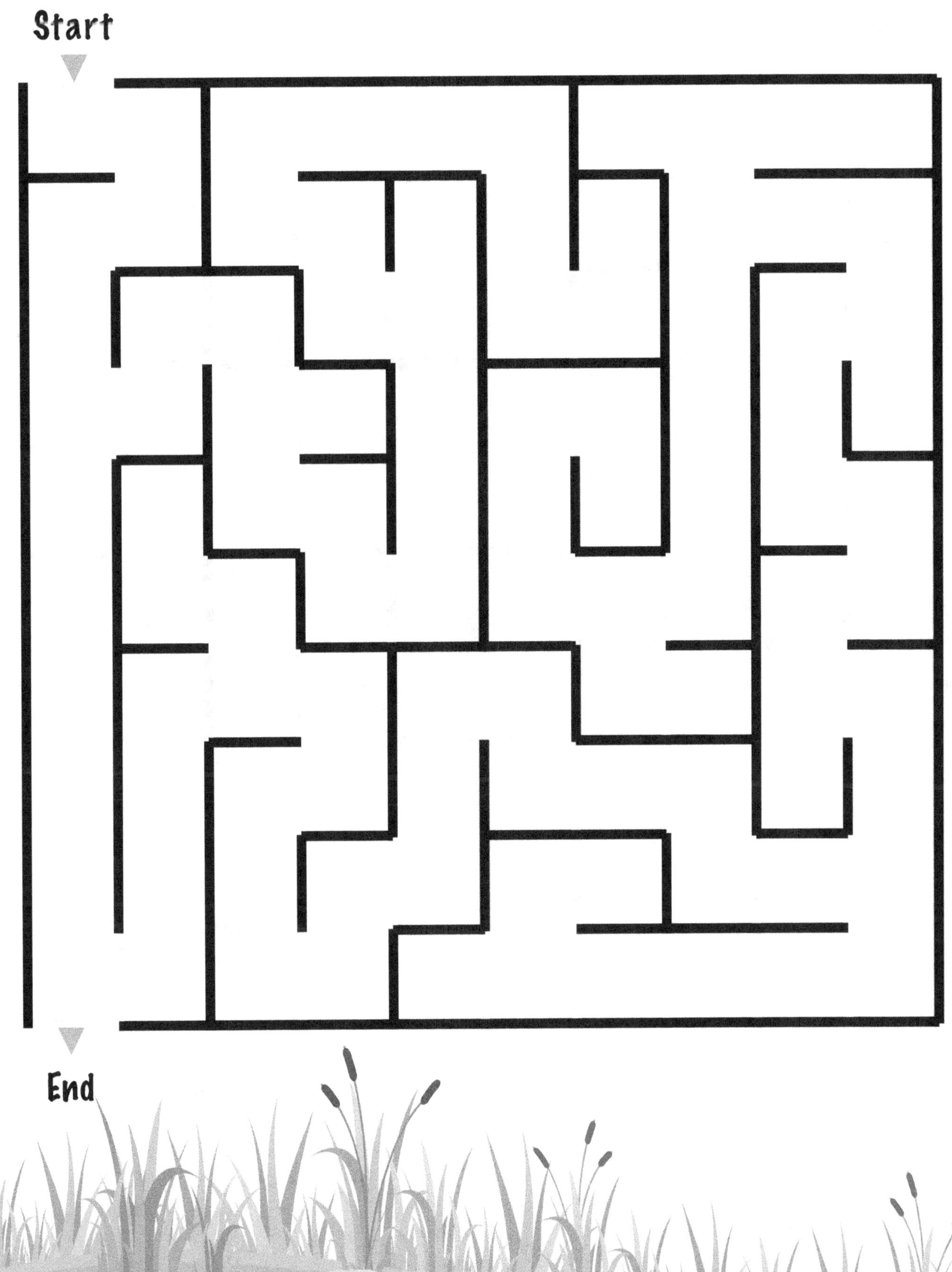

Maze 62

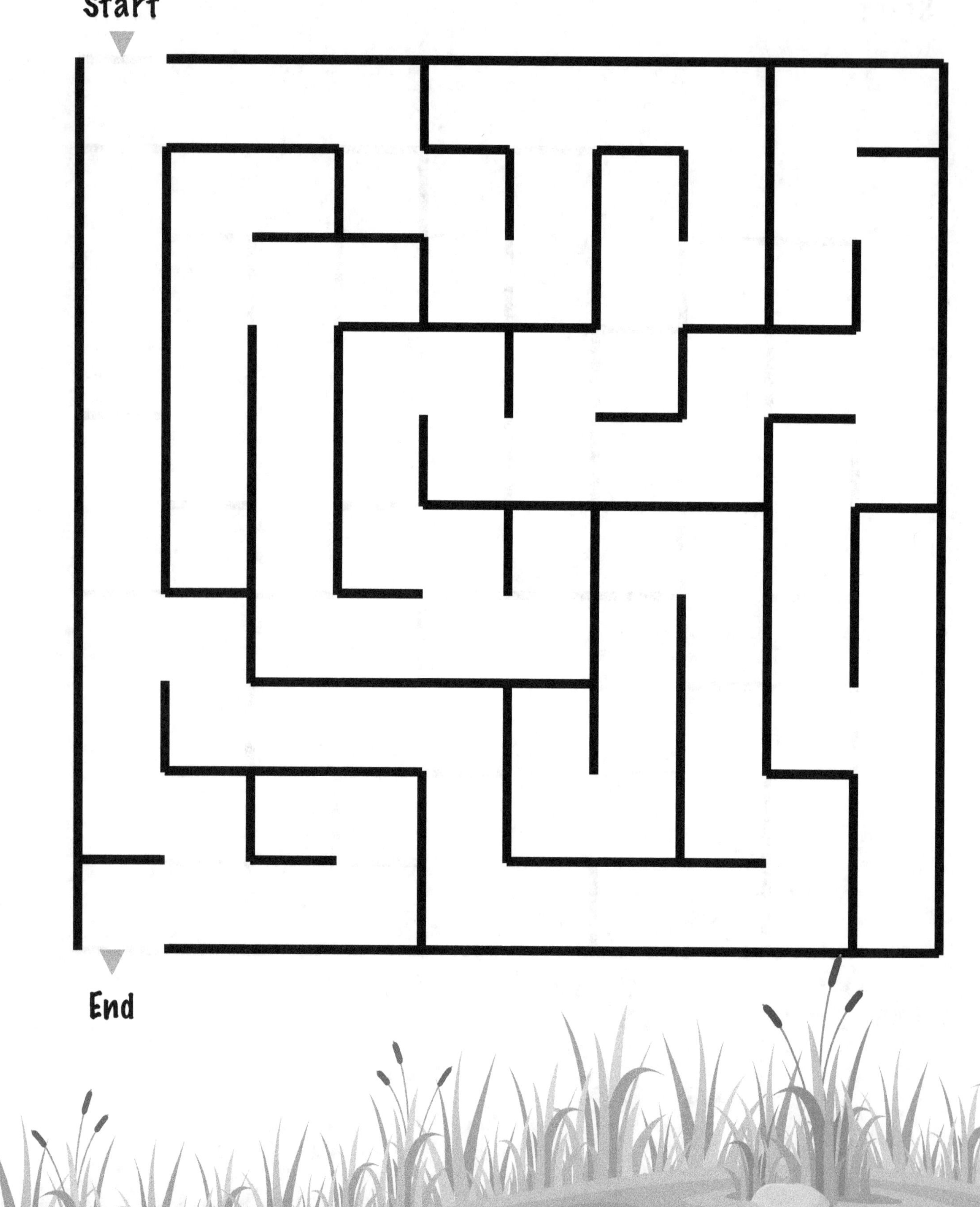

Maze 63

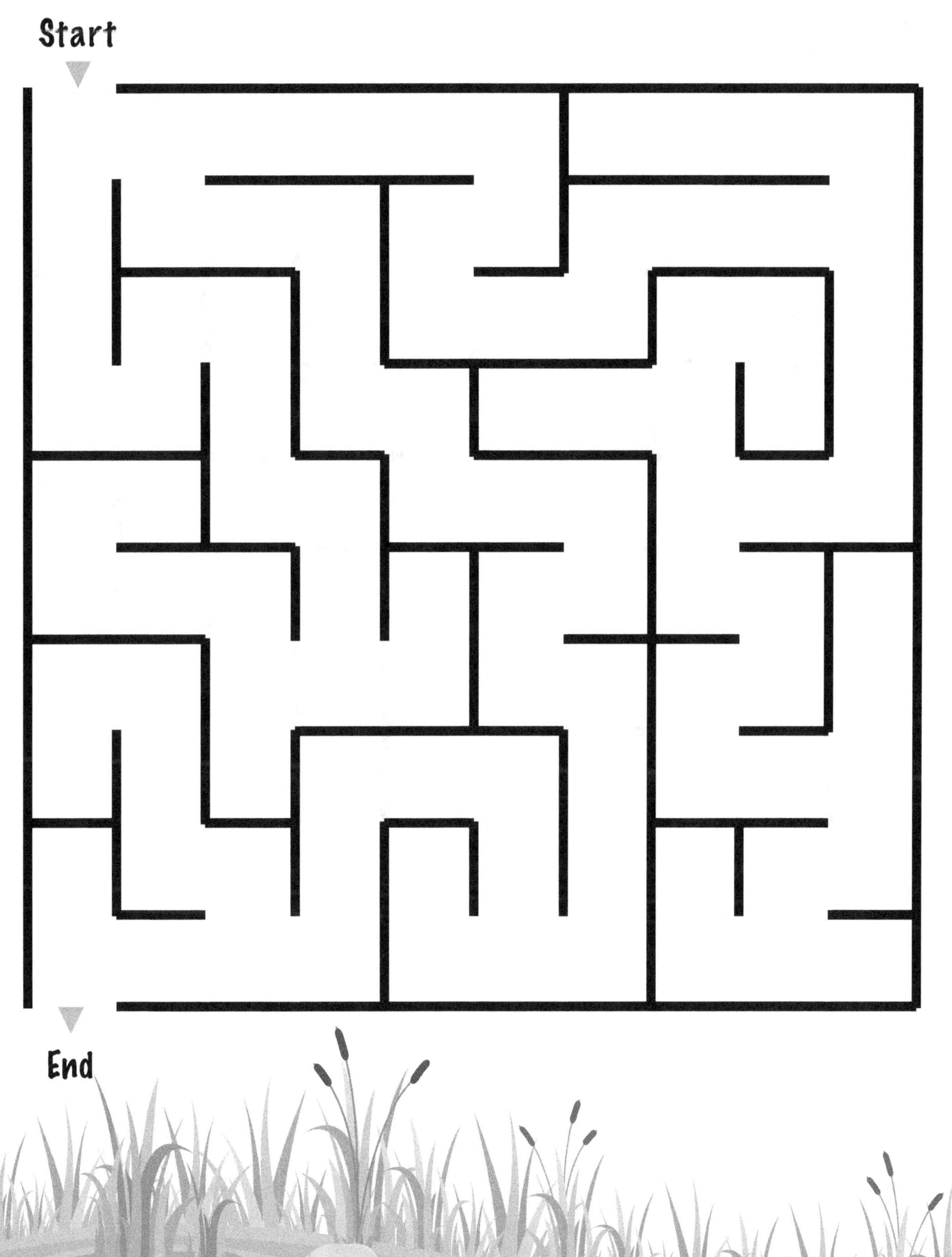

Maze 64

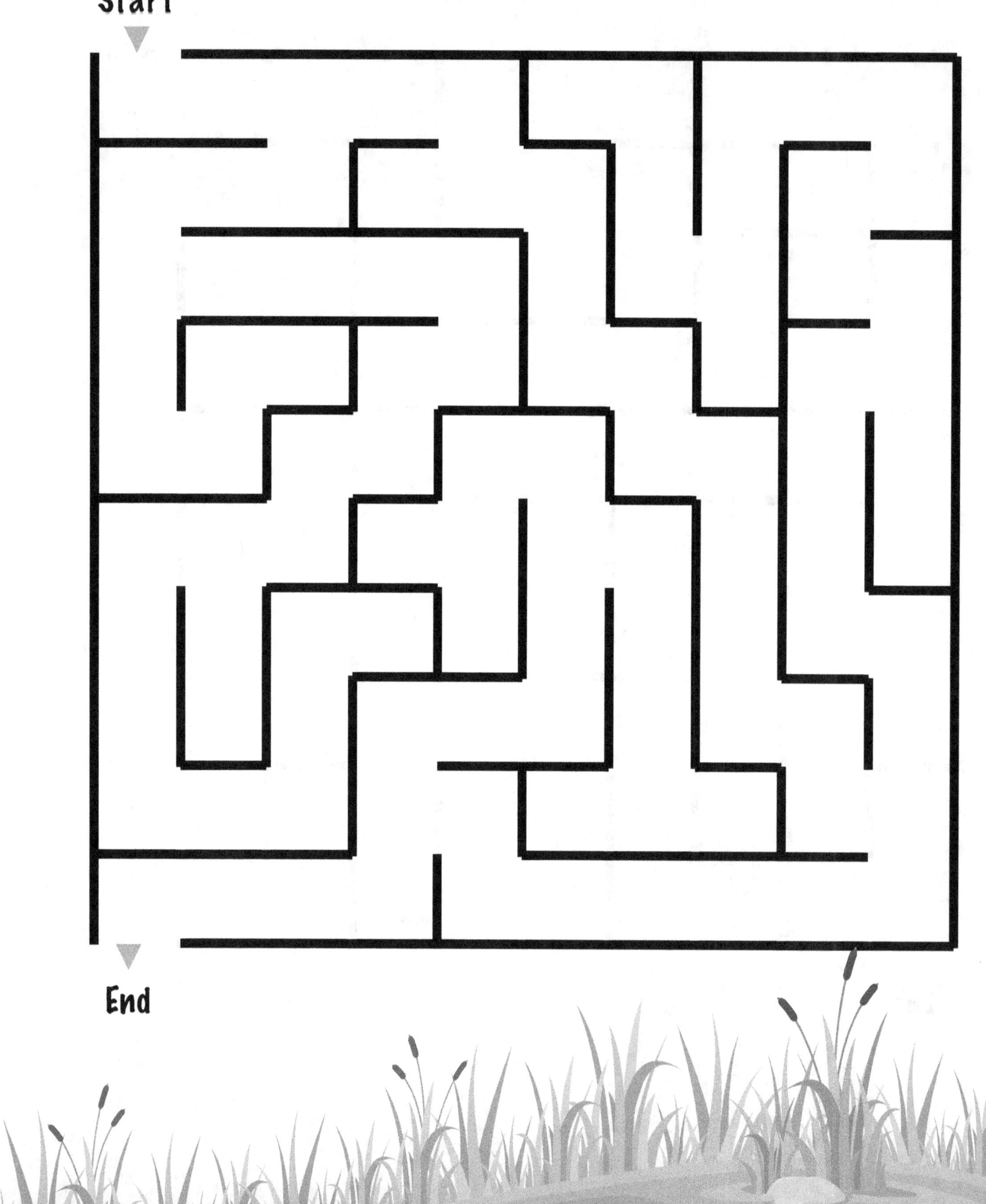

Maze 65

Start

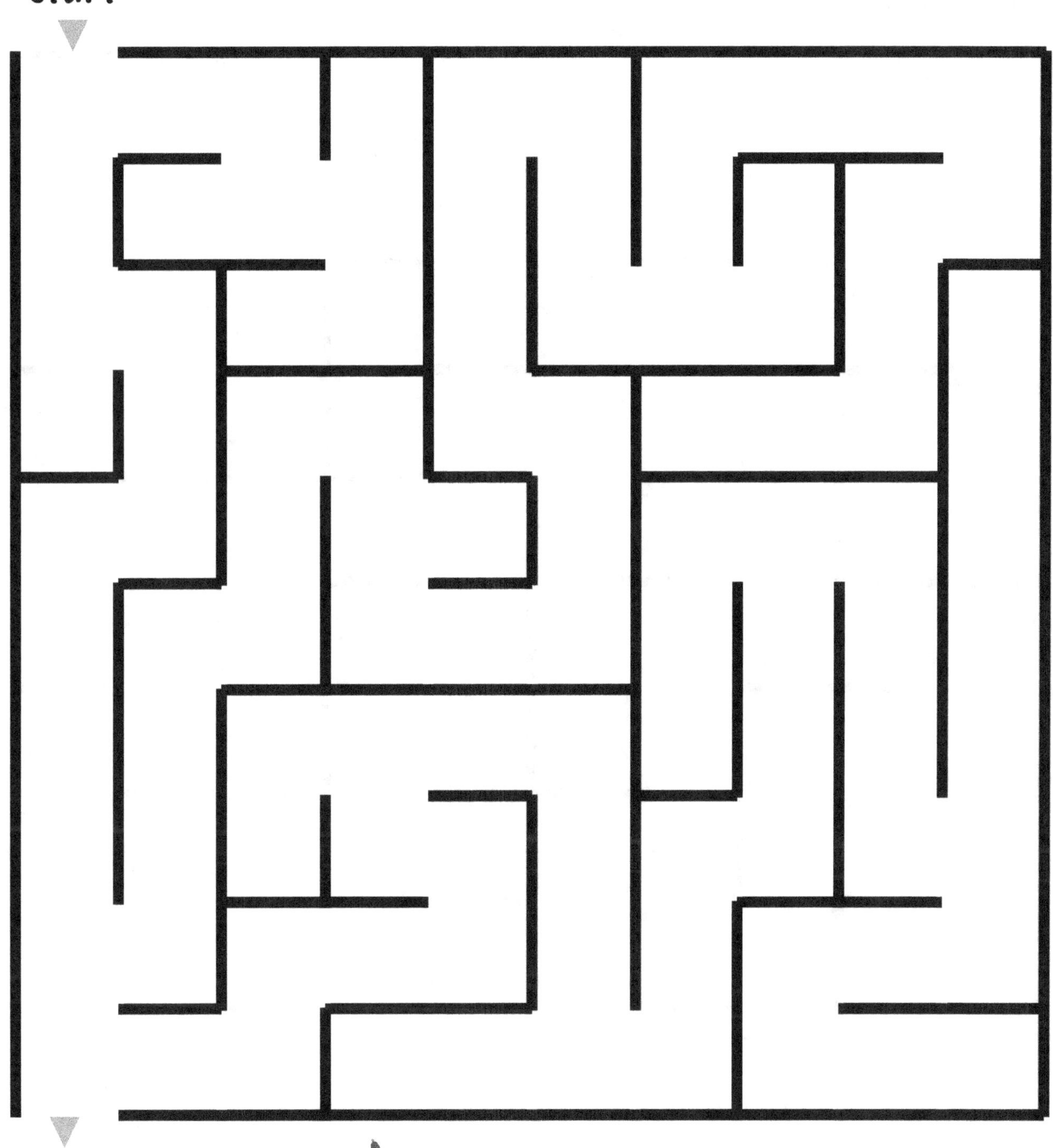

End

Maze 66

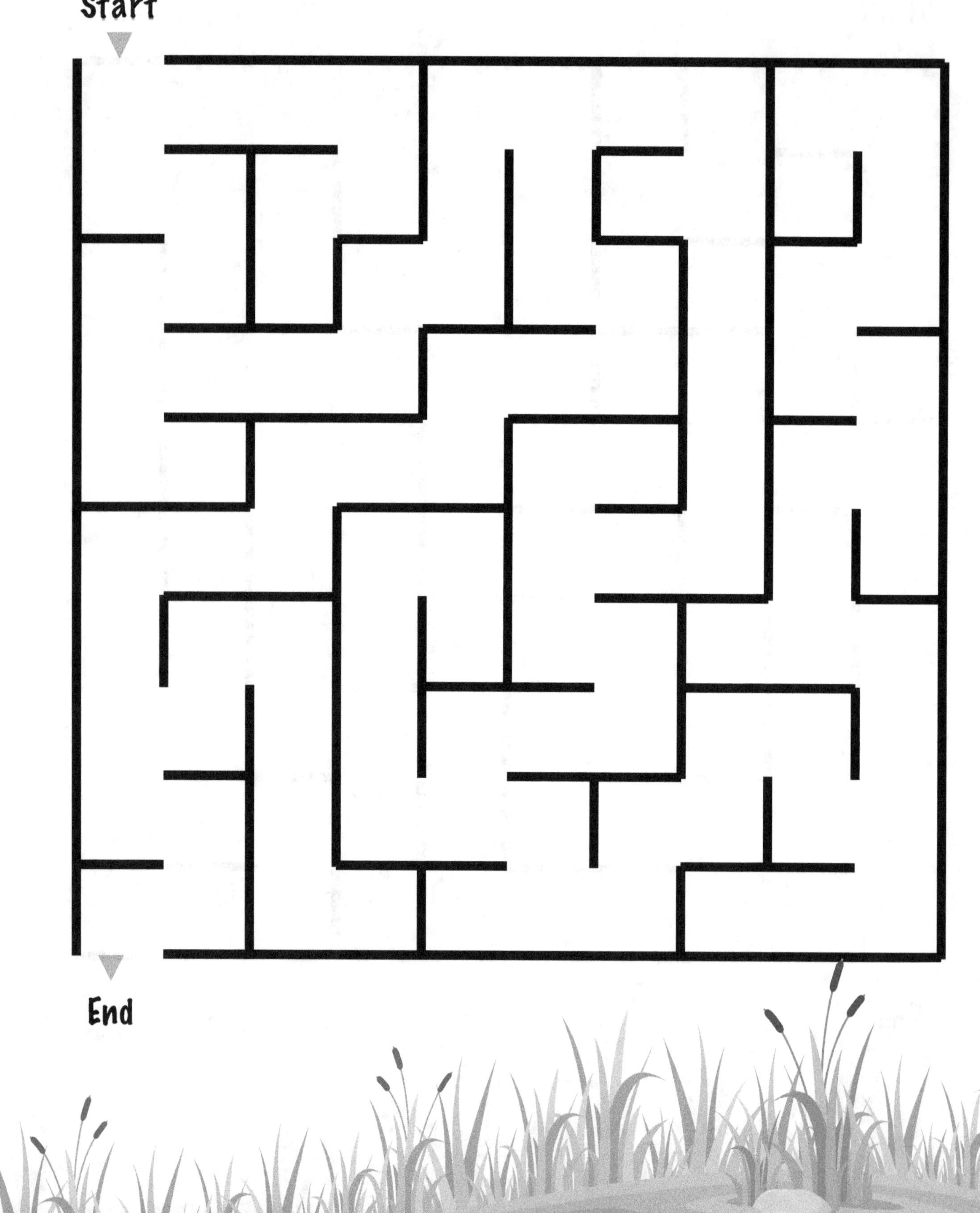

Maze 67

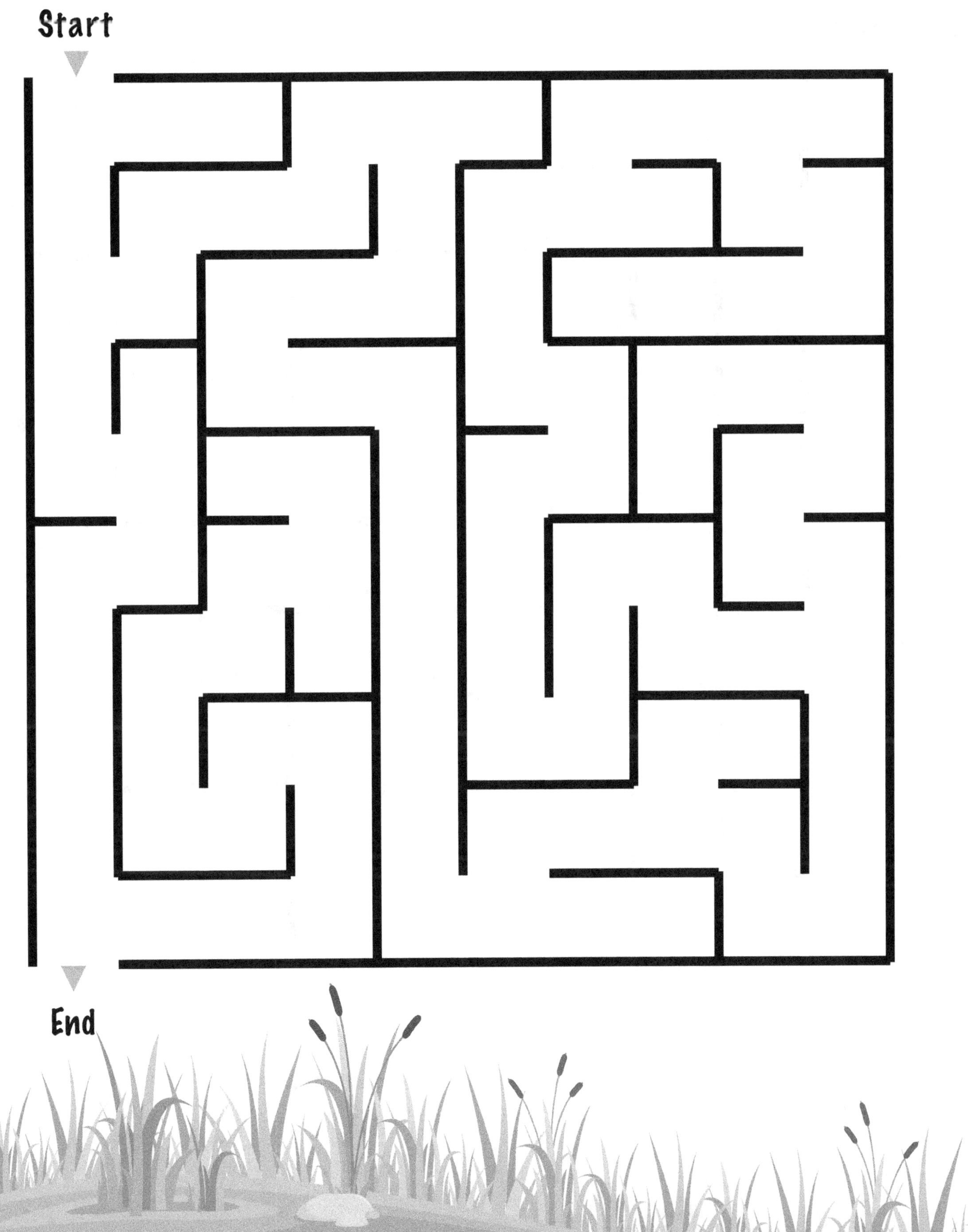

Maze 68

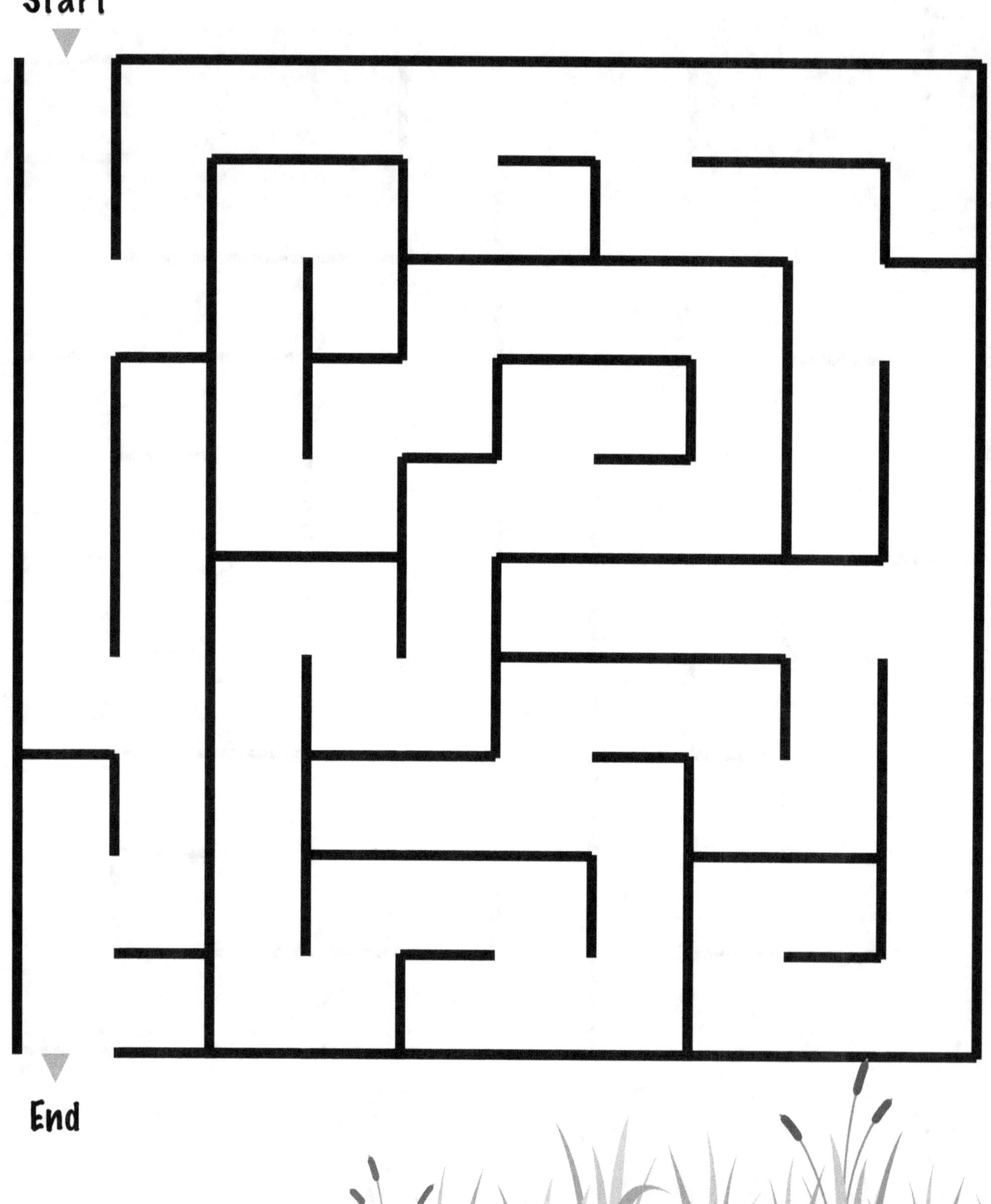

Maze 69

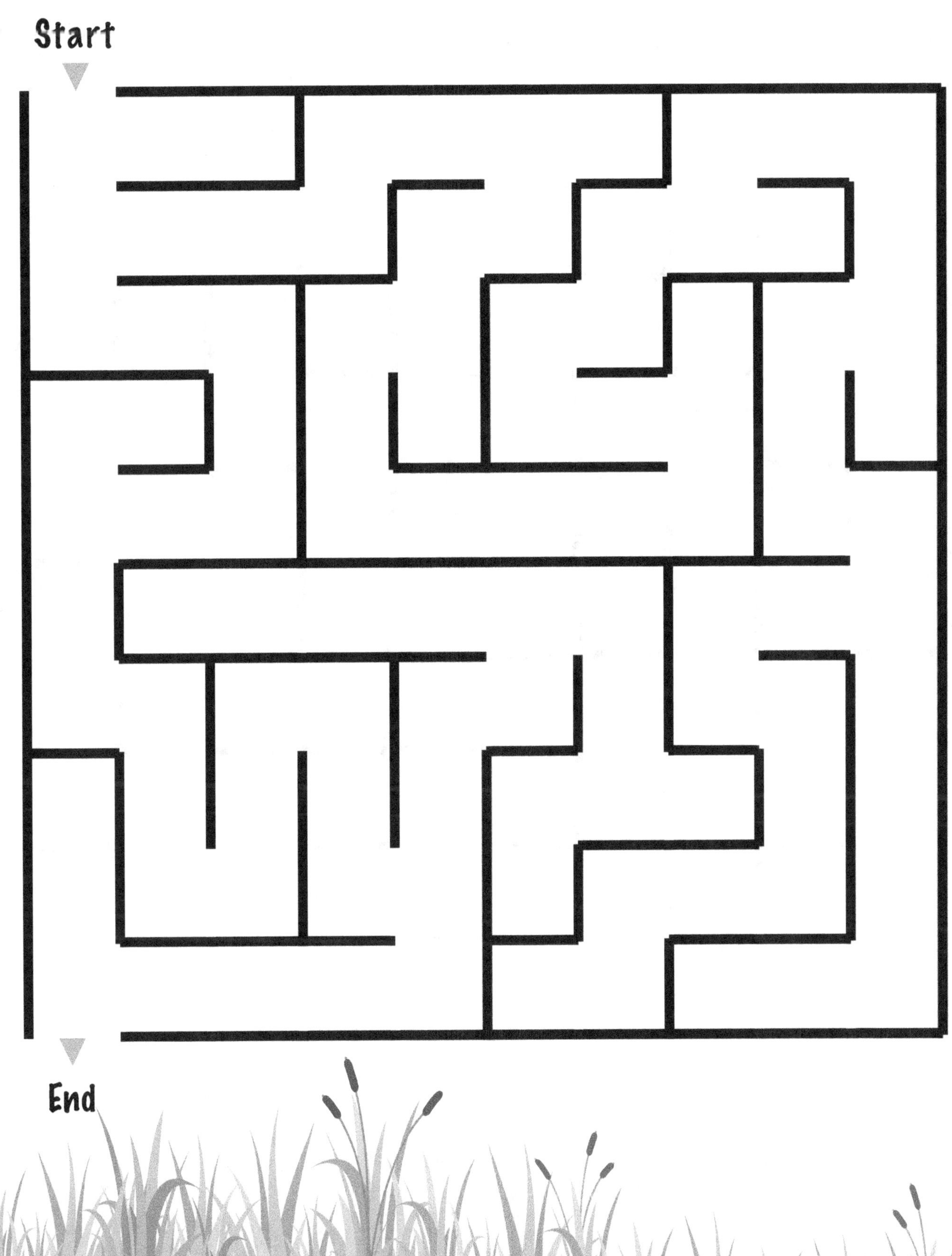

Maze 70

Maze 71

Start

End

Maze 72

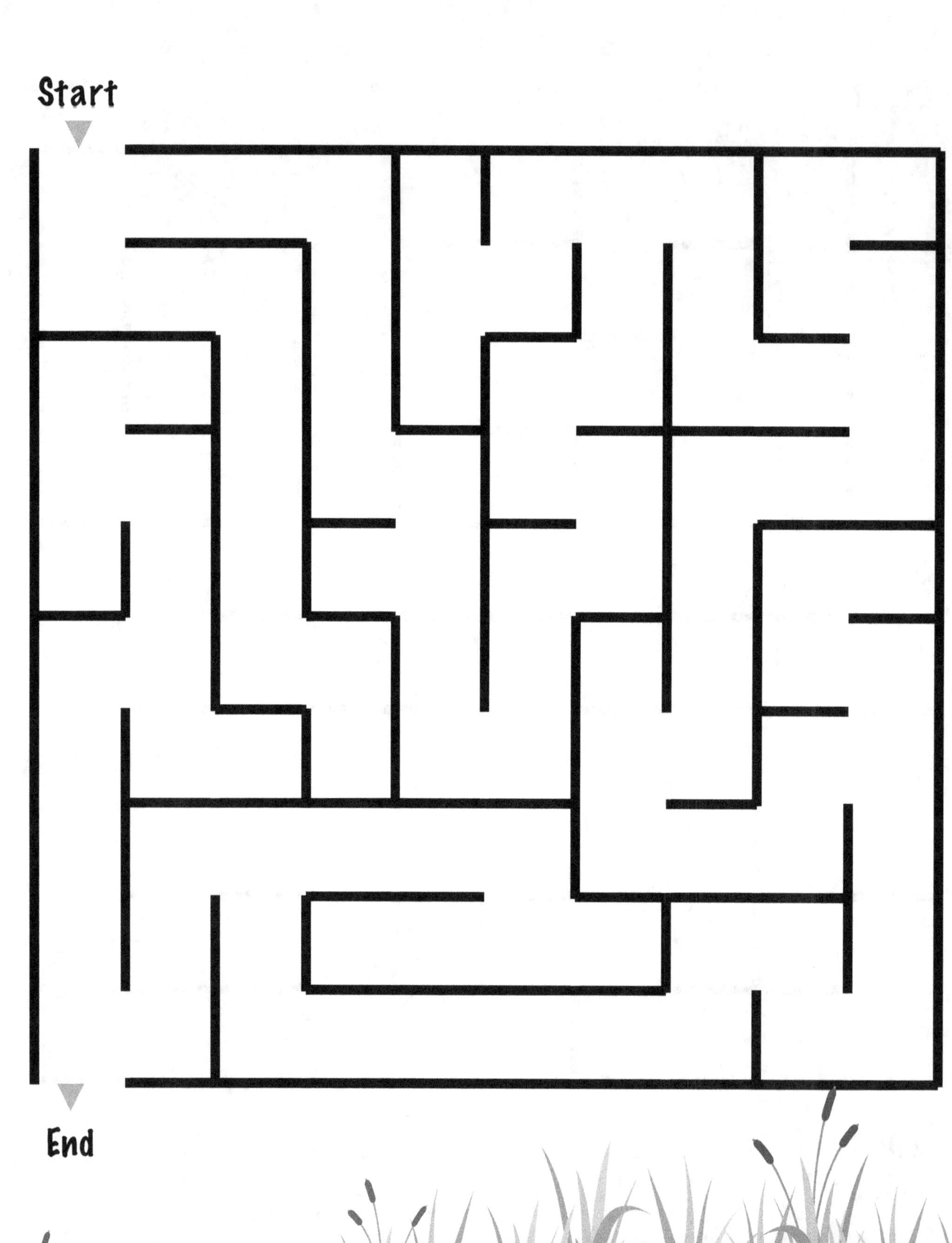

Maze 73

Start

End

Maze 74

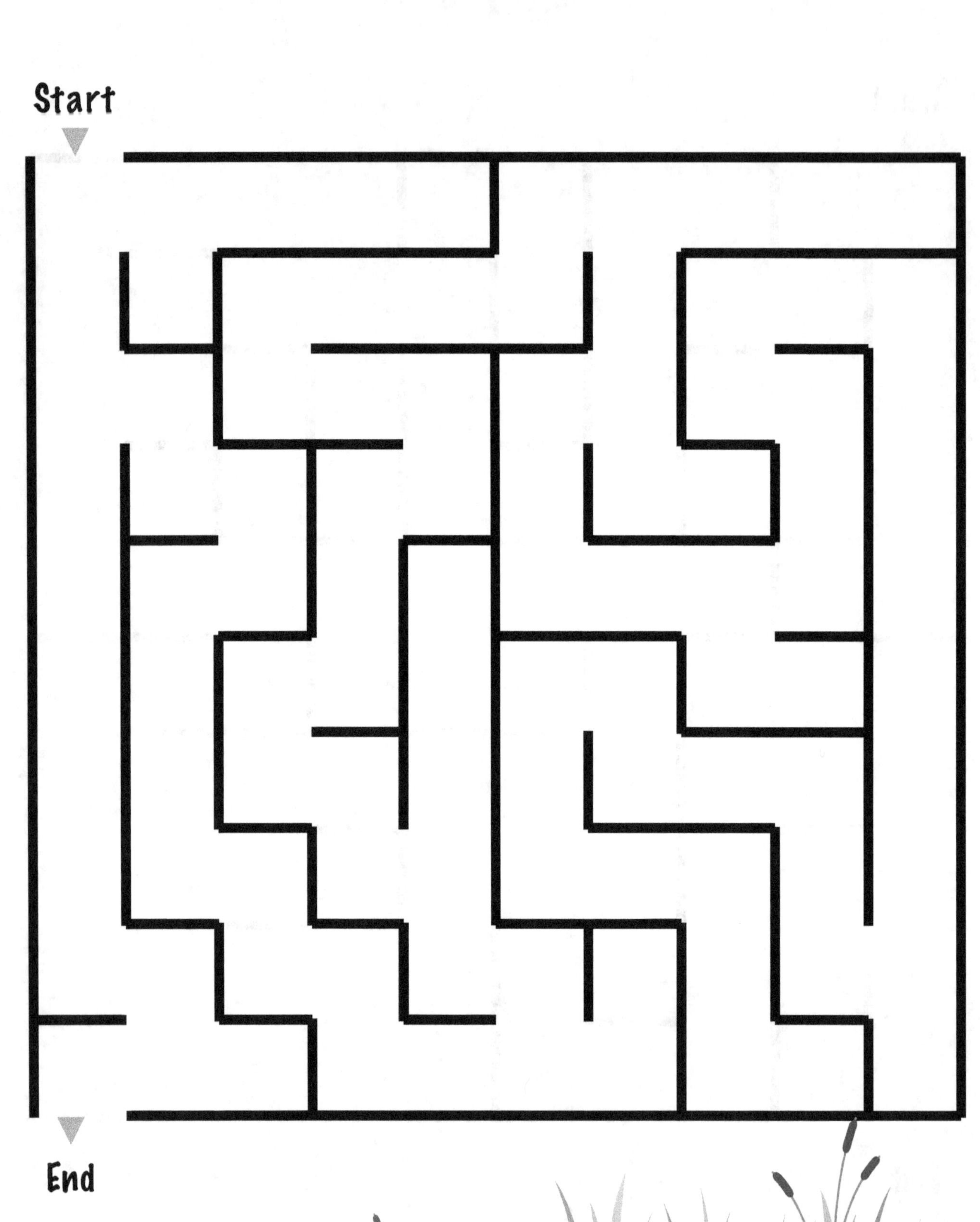

Maze 75

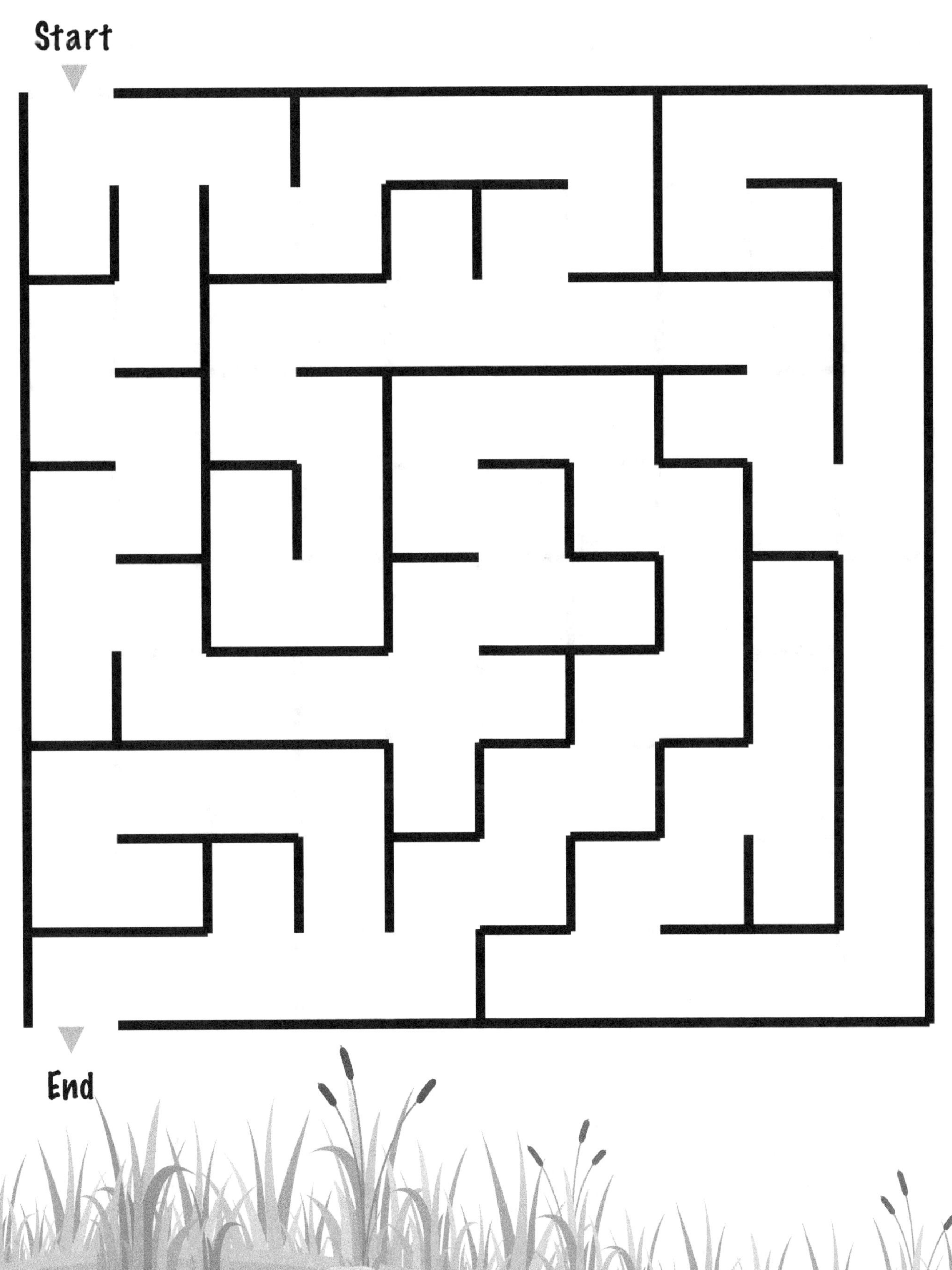

Maze 76

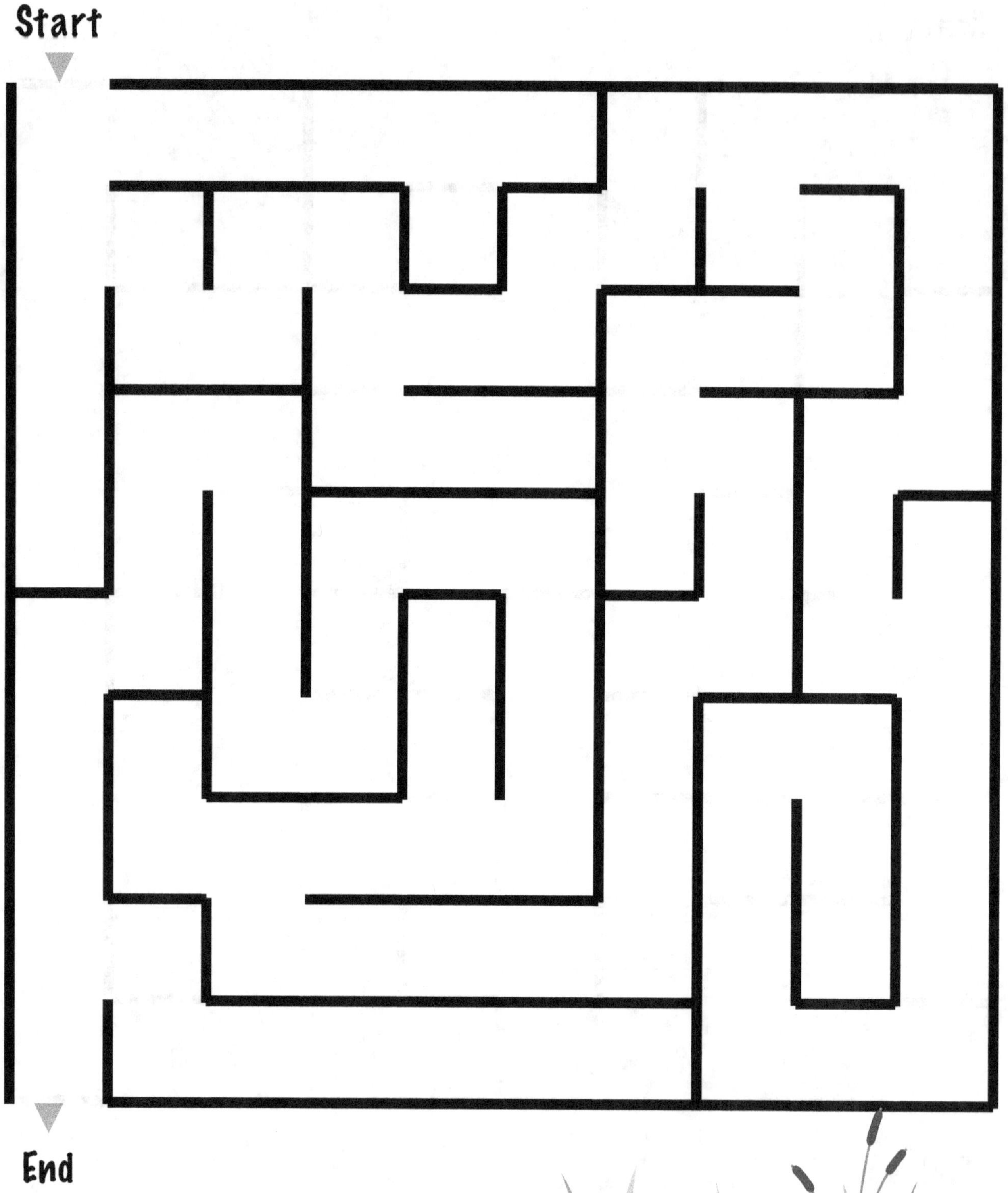

Start

End

Maze 77

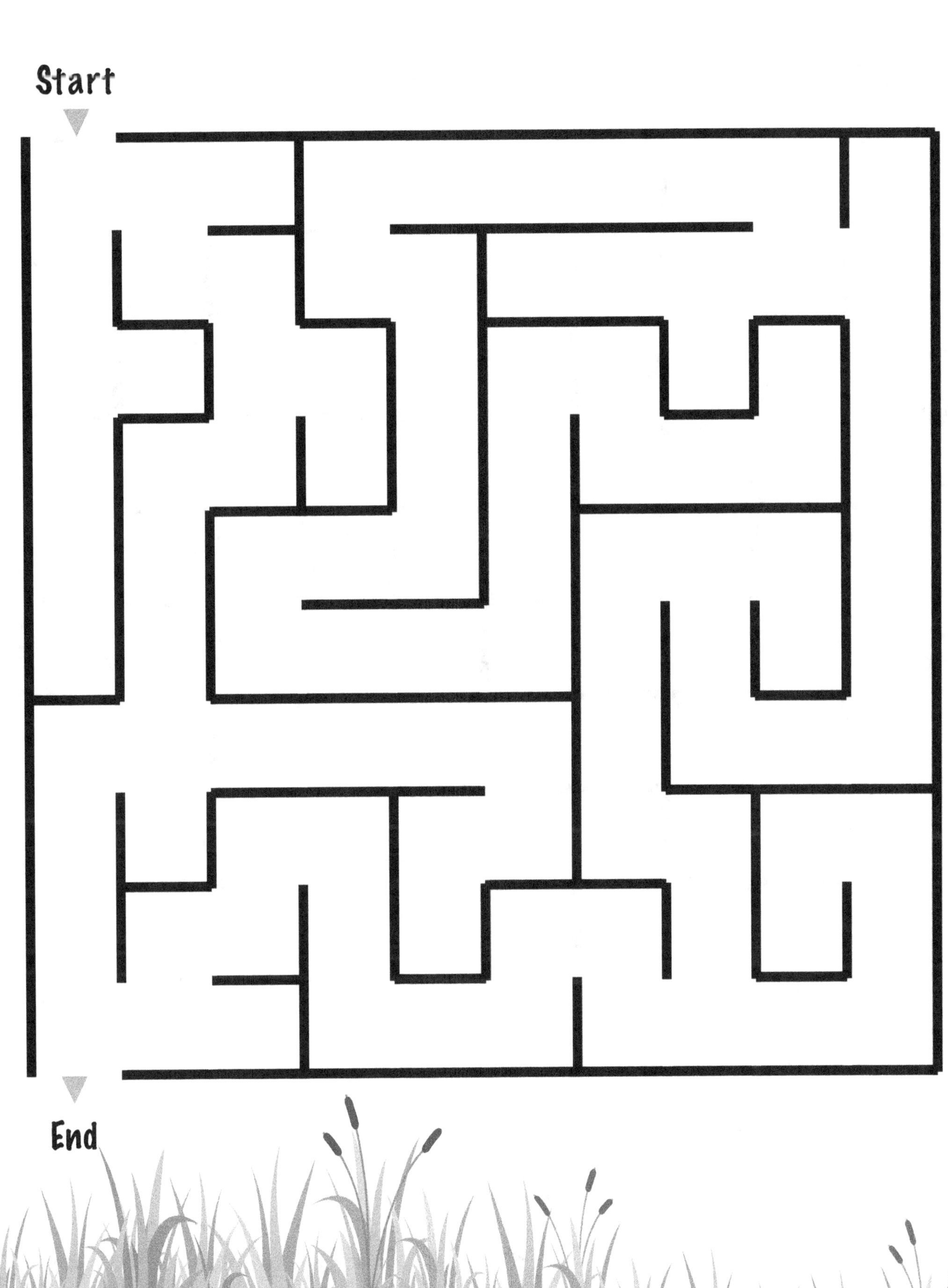

Maze 78

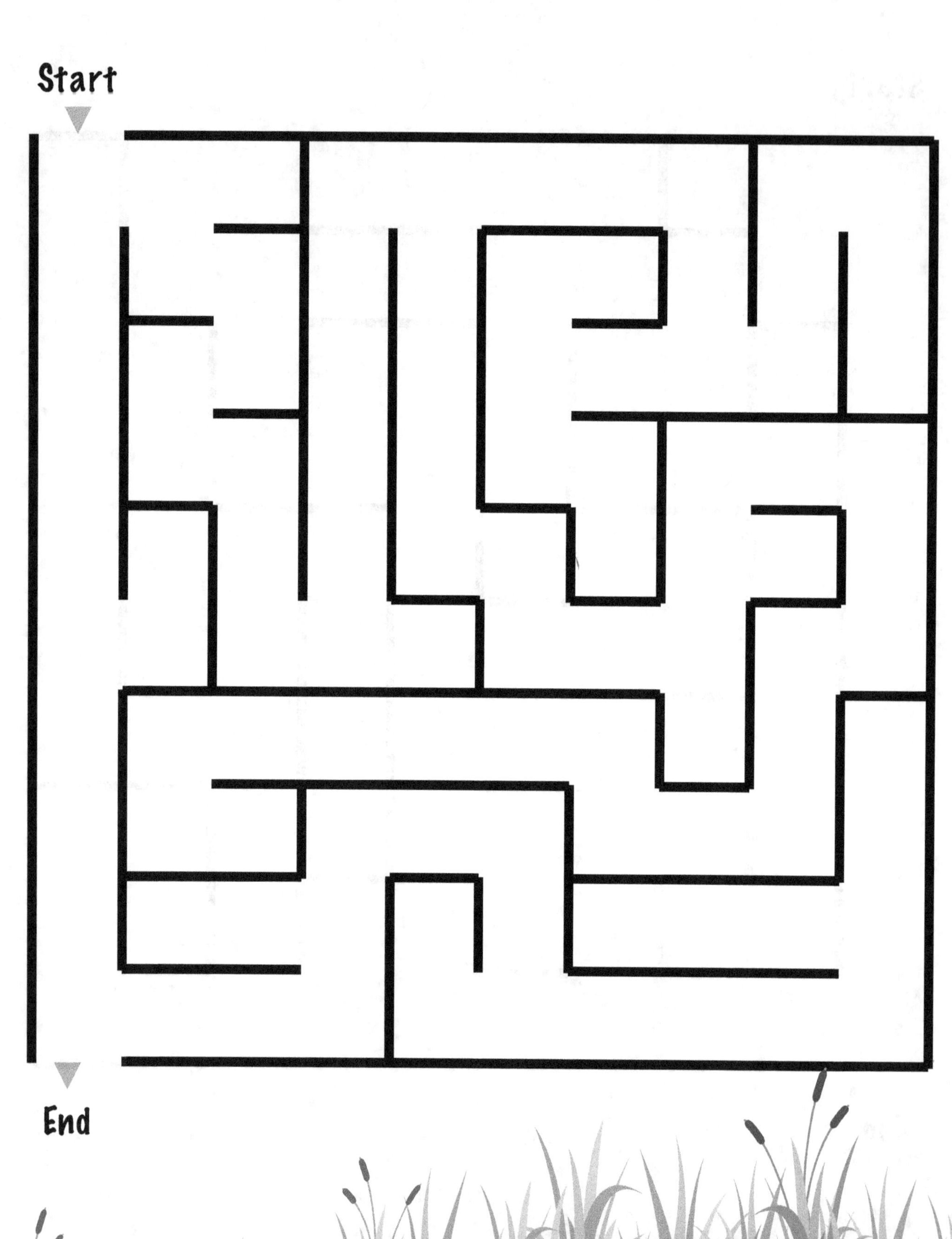

Maze 79

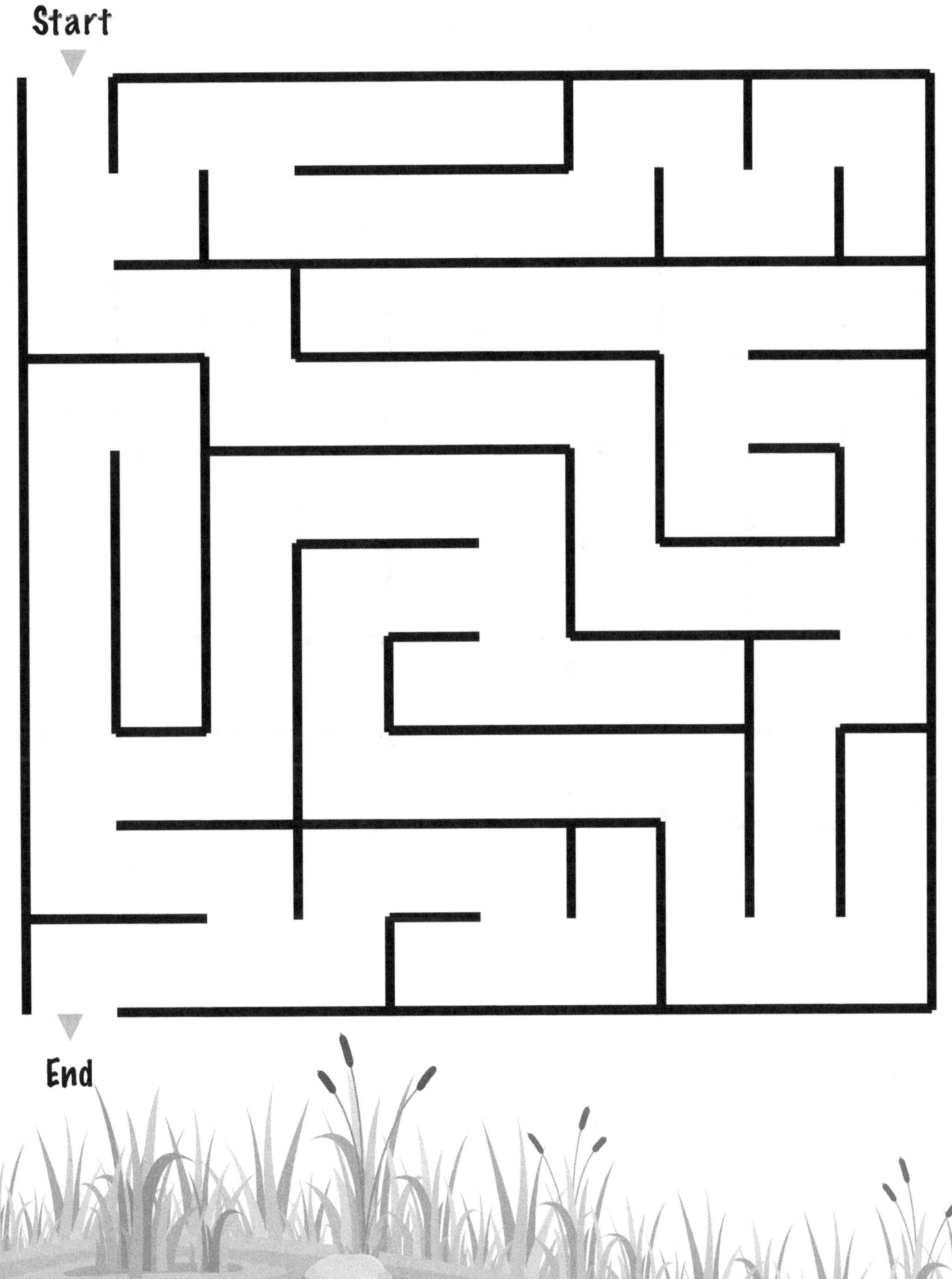

Maze 80

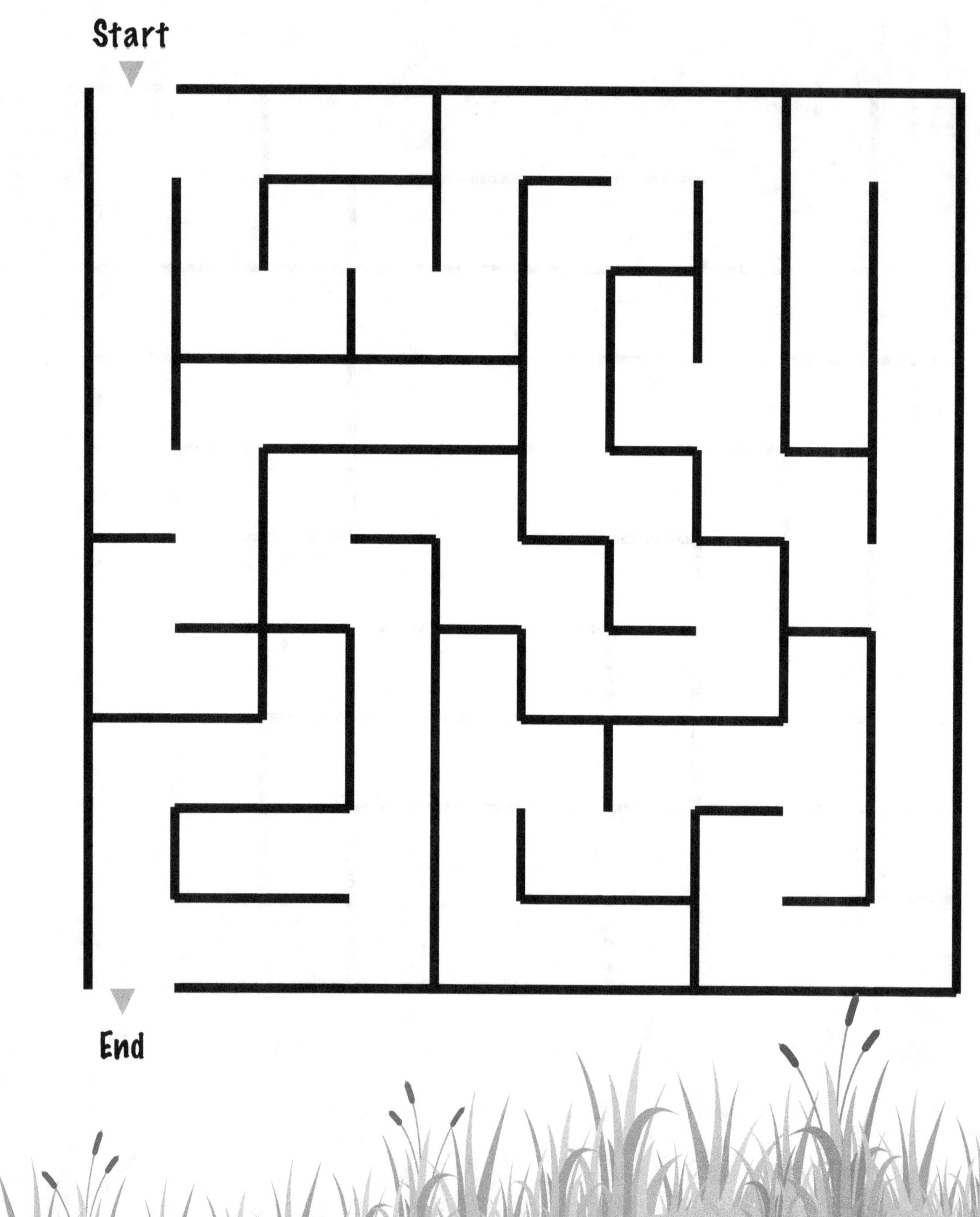

Maze 81

Maze 82

Maze 83

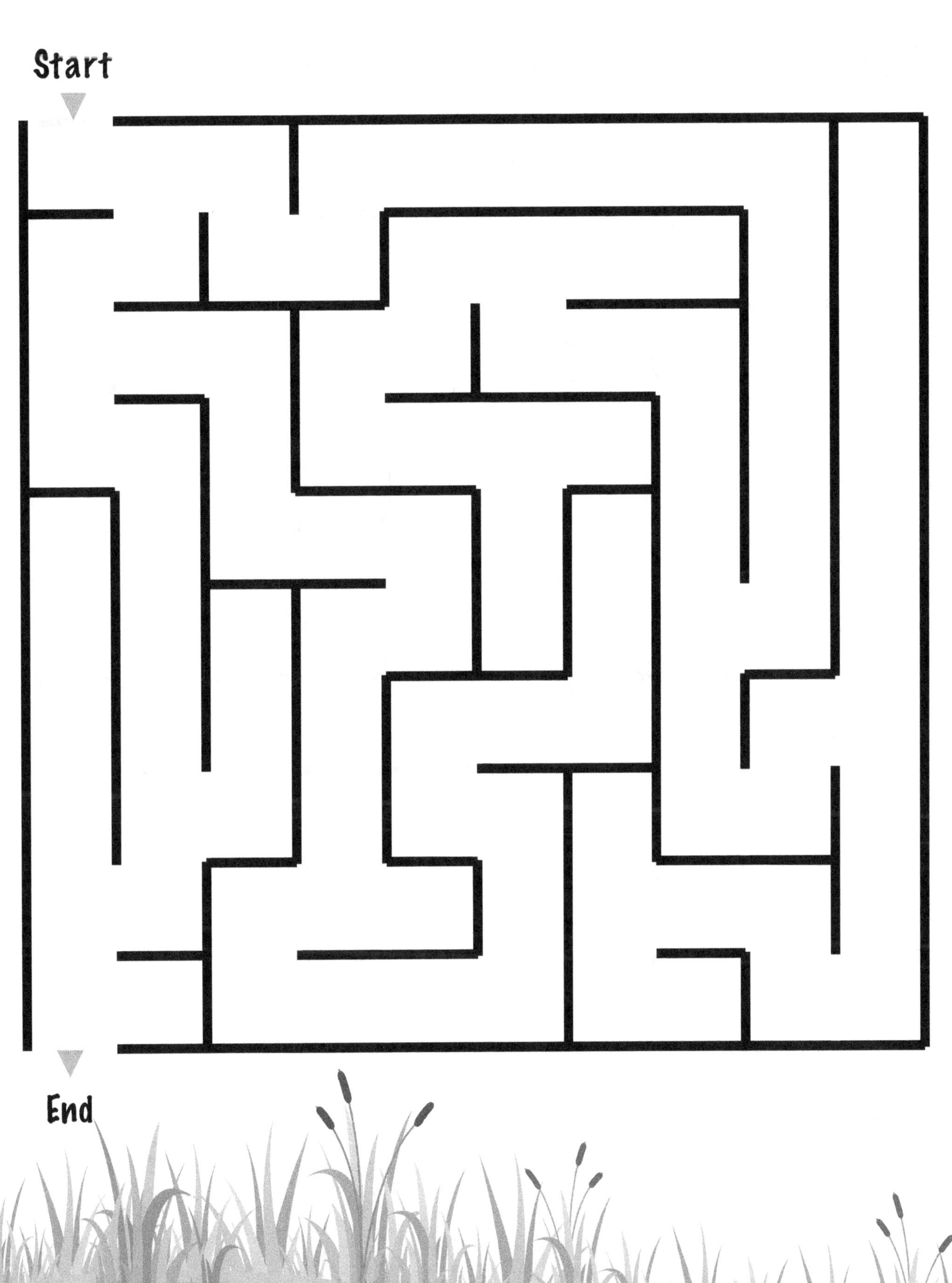

Maze 84

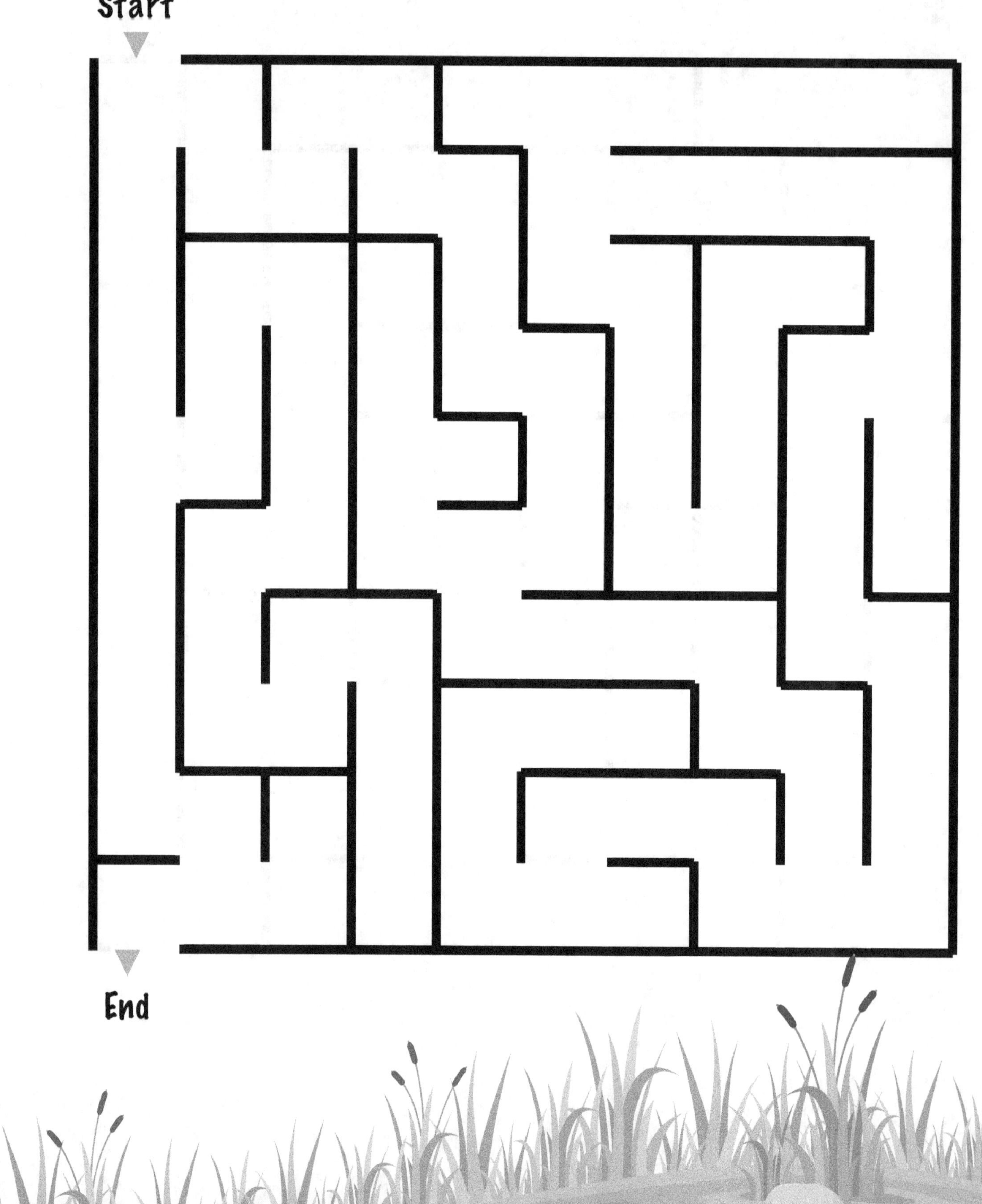

Maze 85

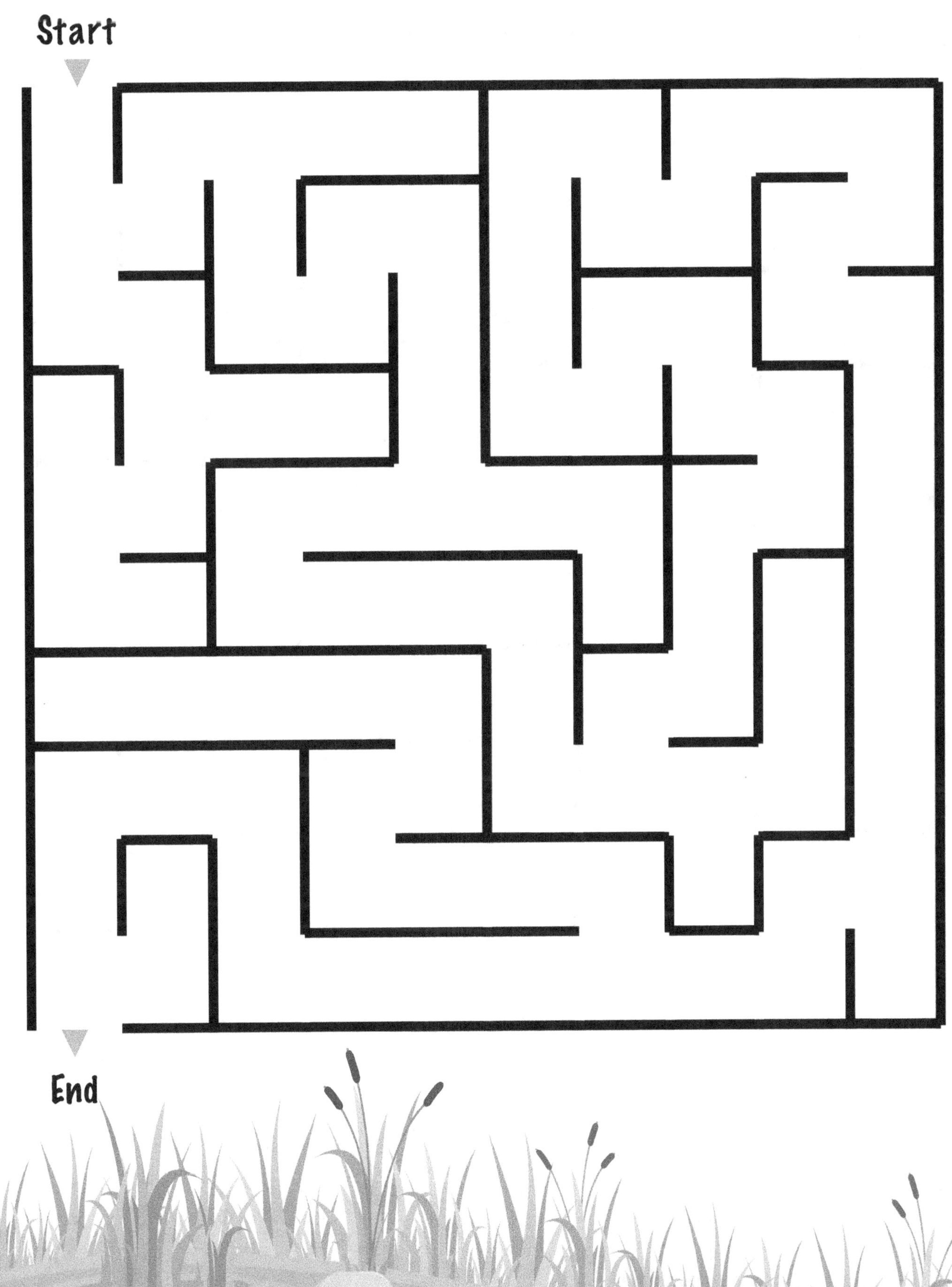

Maze 86

Maze 87

Maze 88

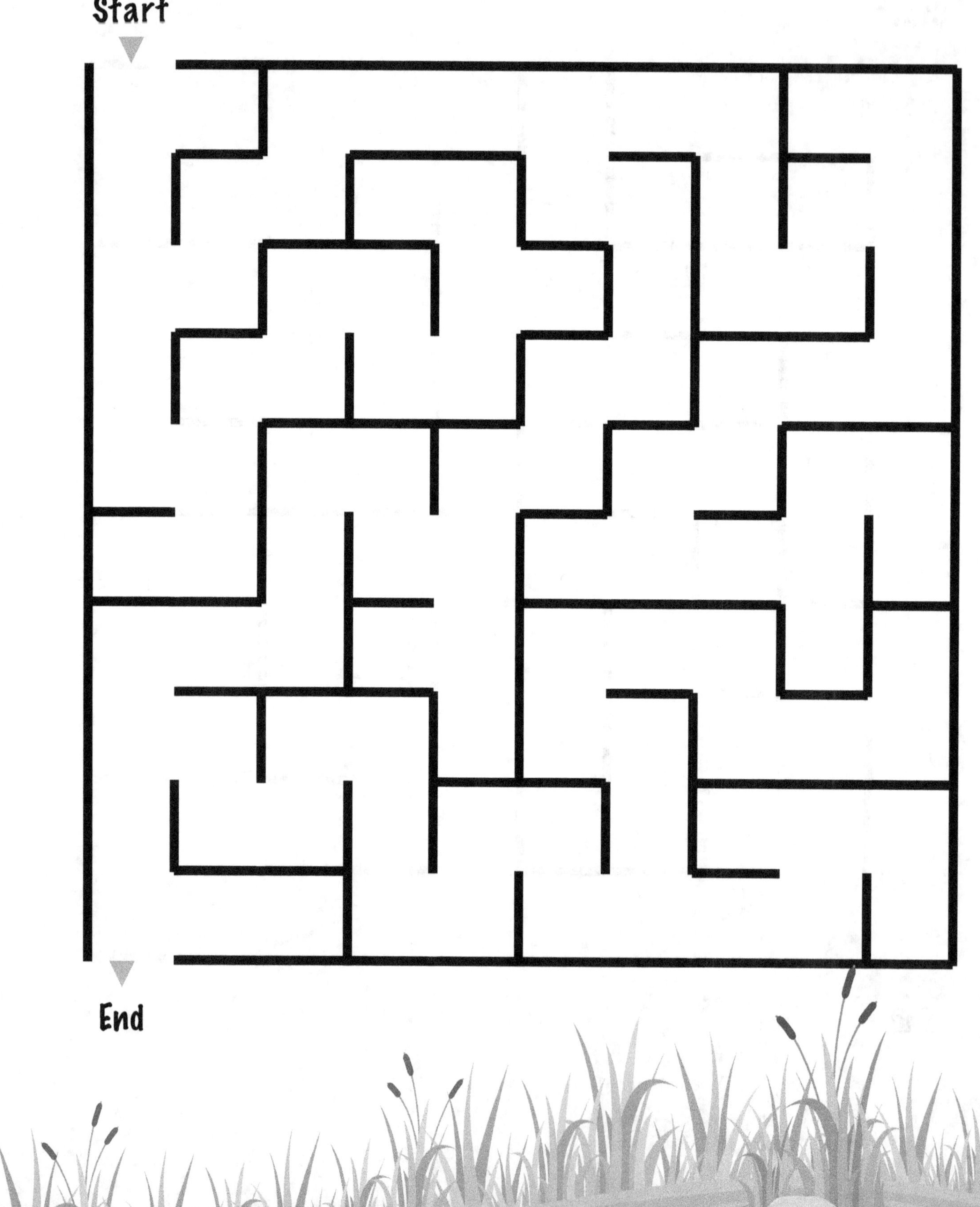

Maze 89

Maze 90

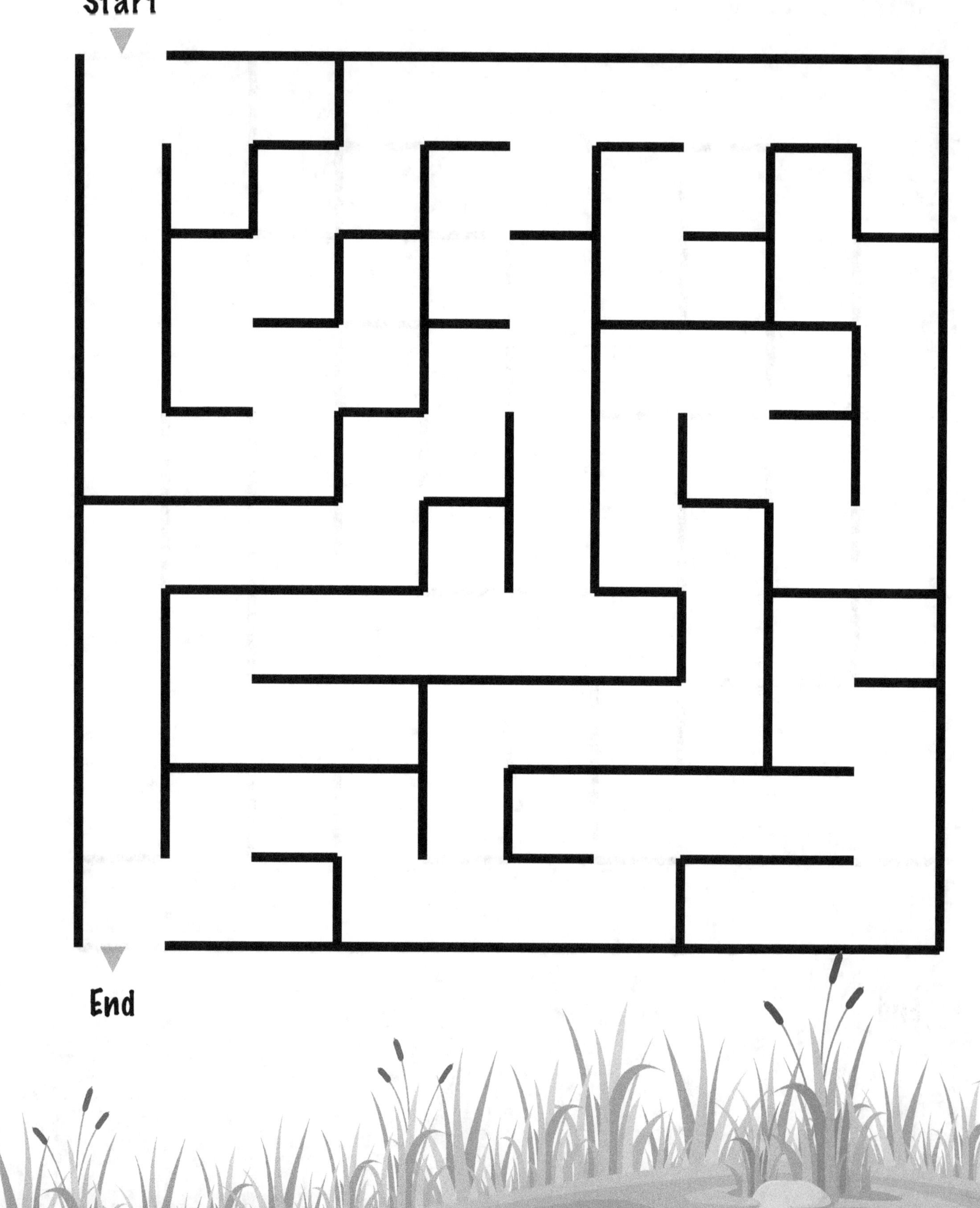

Maze 91

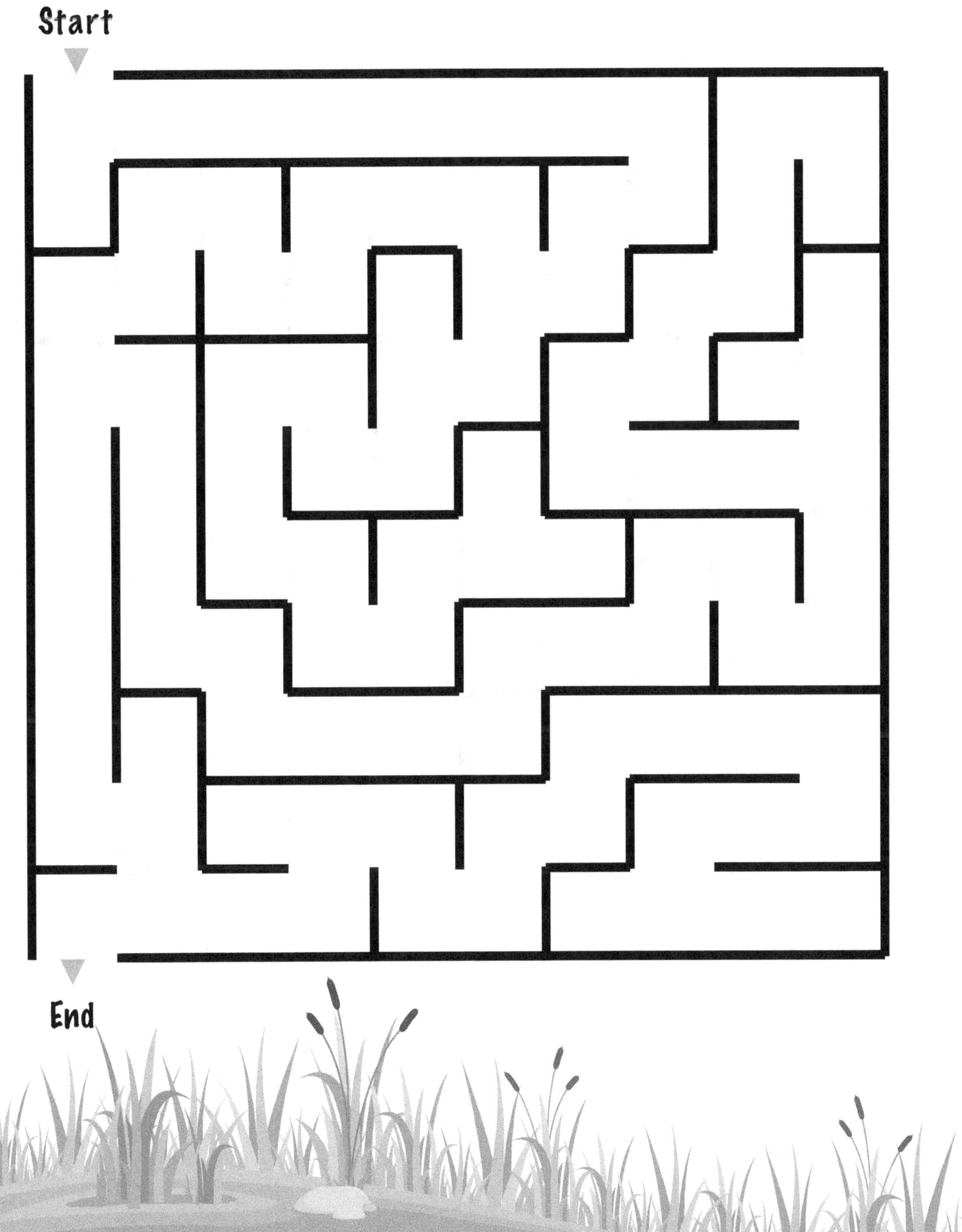

Maze 92

Maze 93

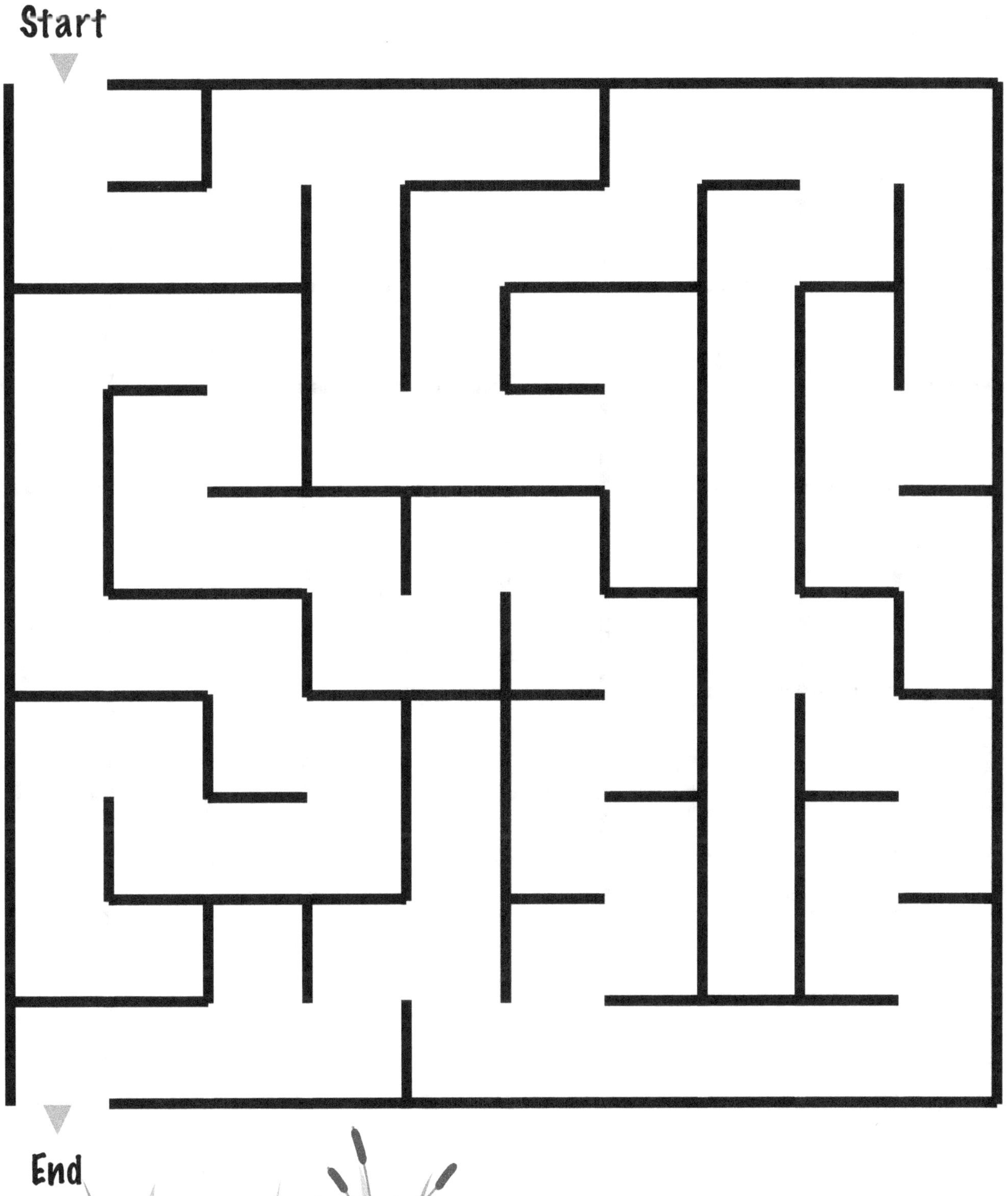

Start

End

Maze 94

Maze 95

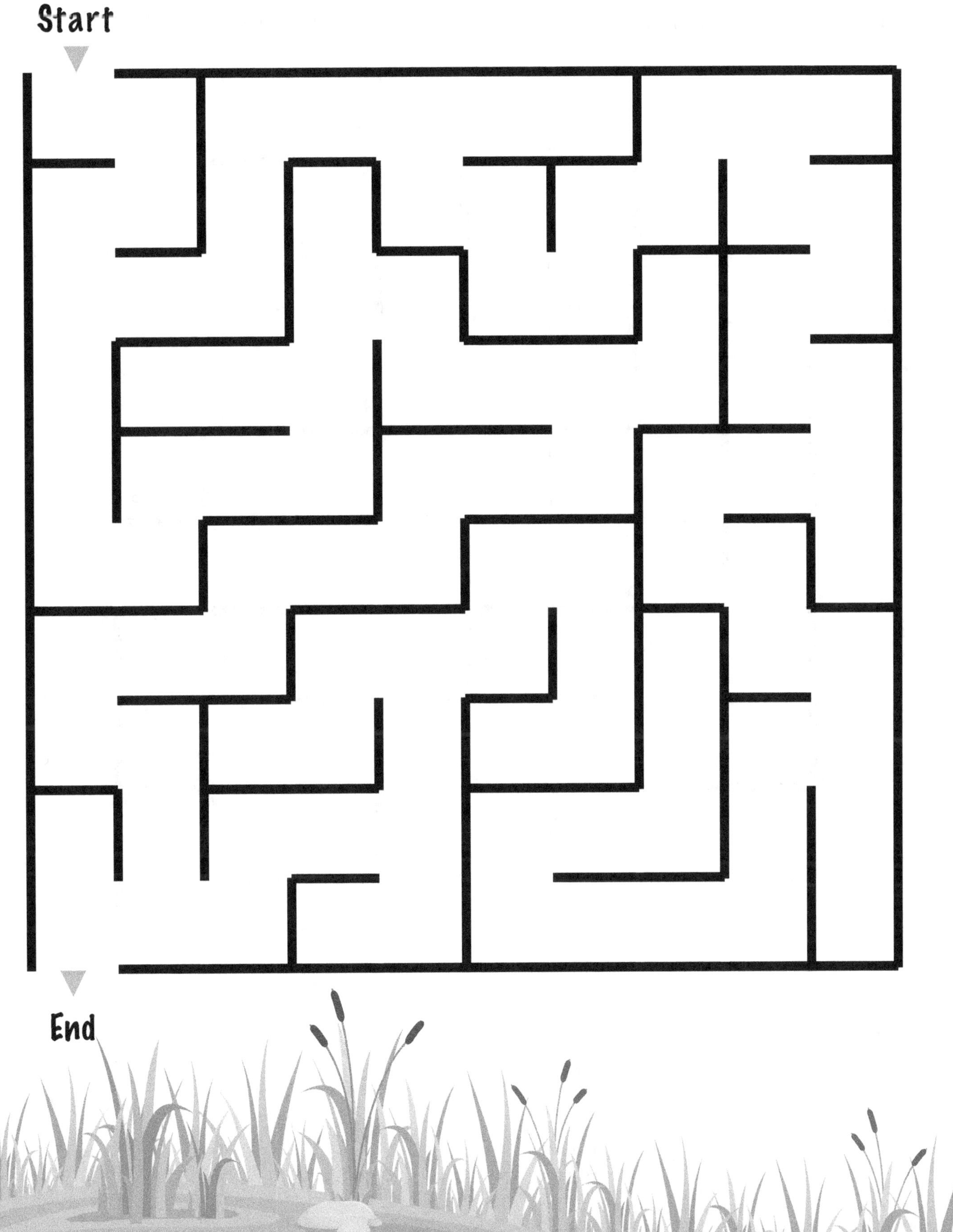

Maze 96

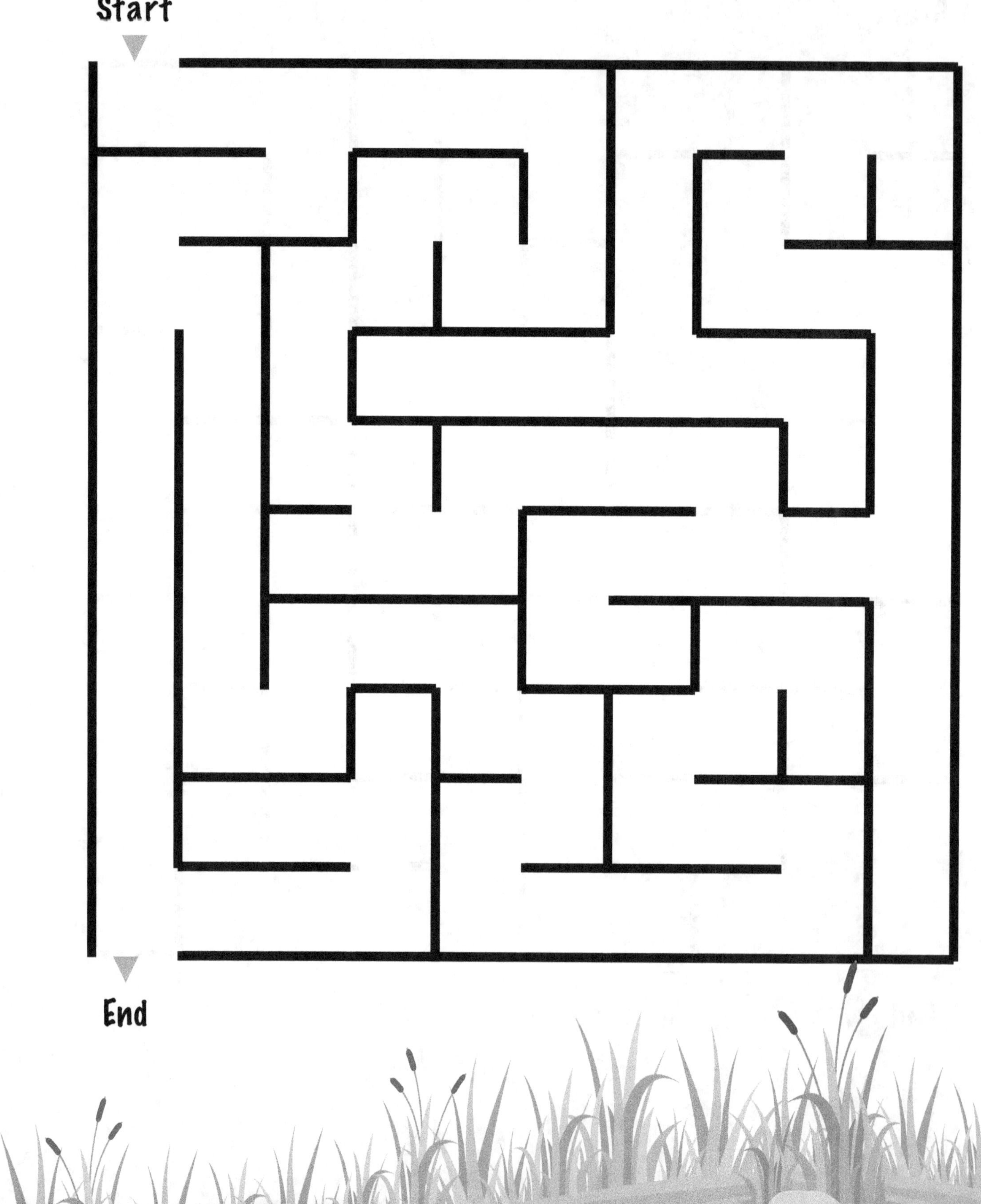

Maze 97

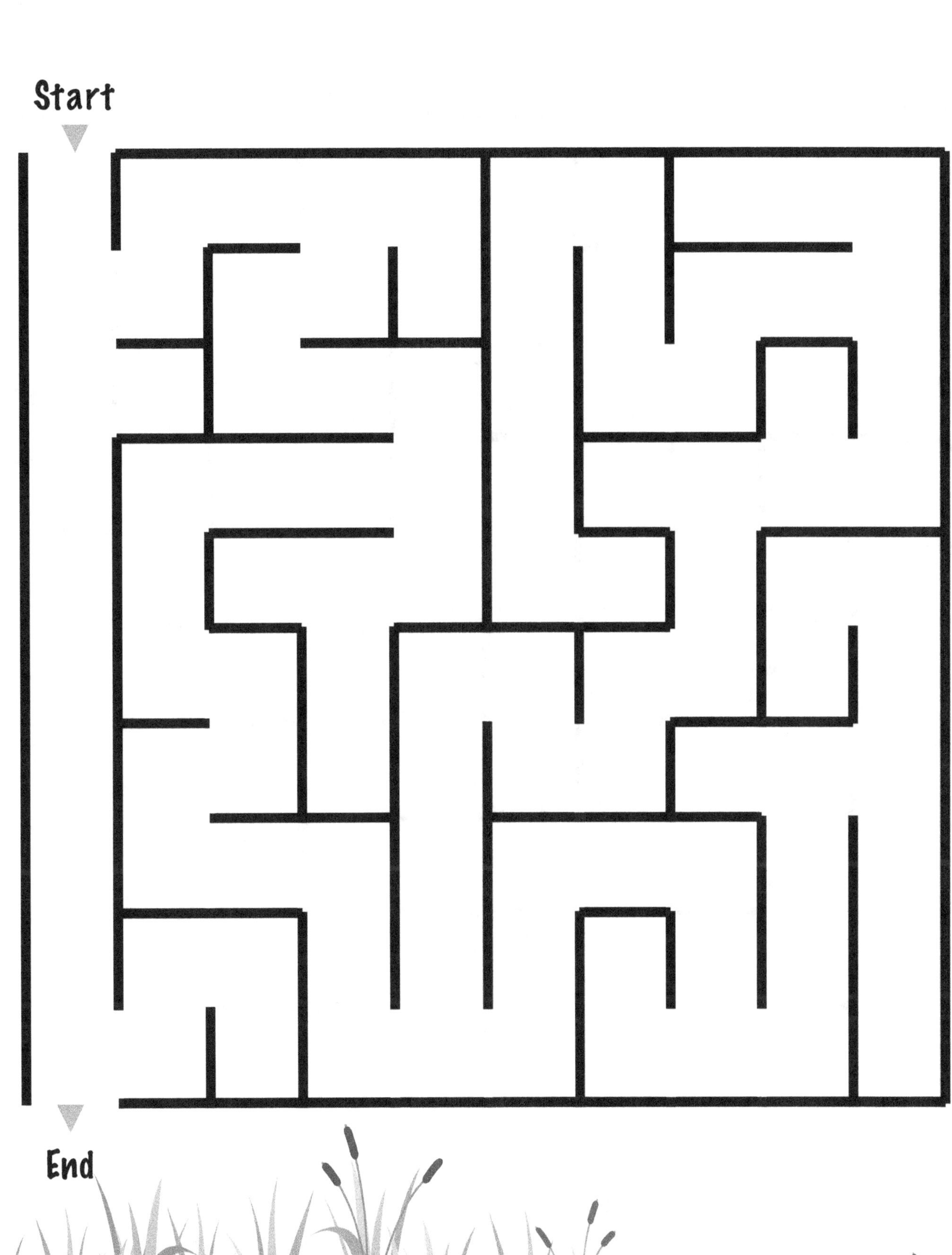

Maze 98

Maze 99

Start

End

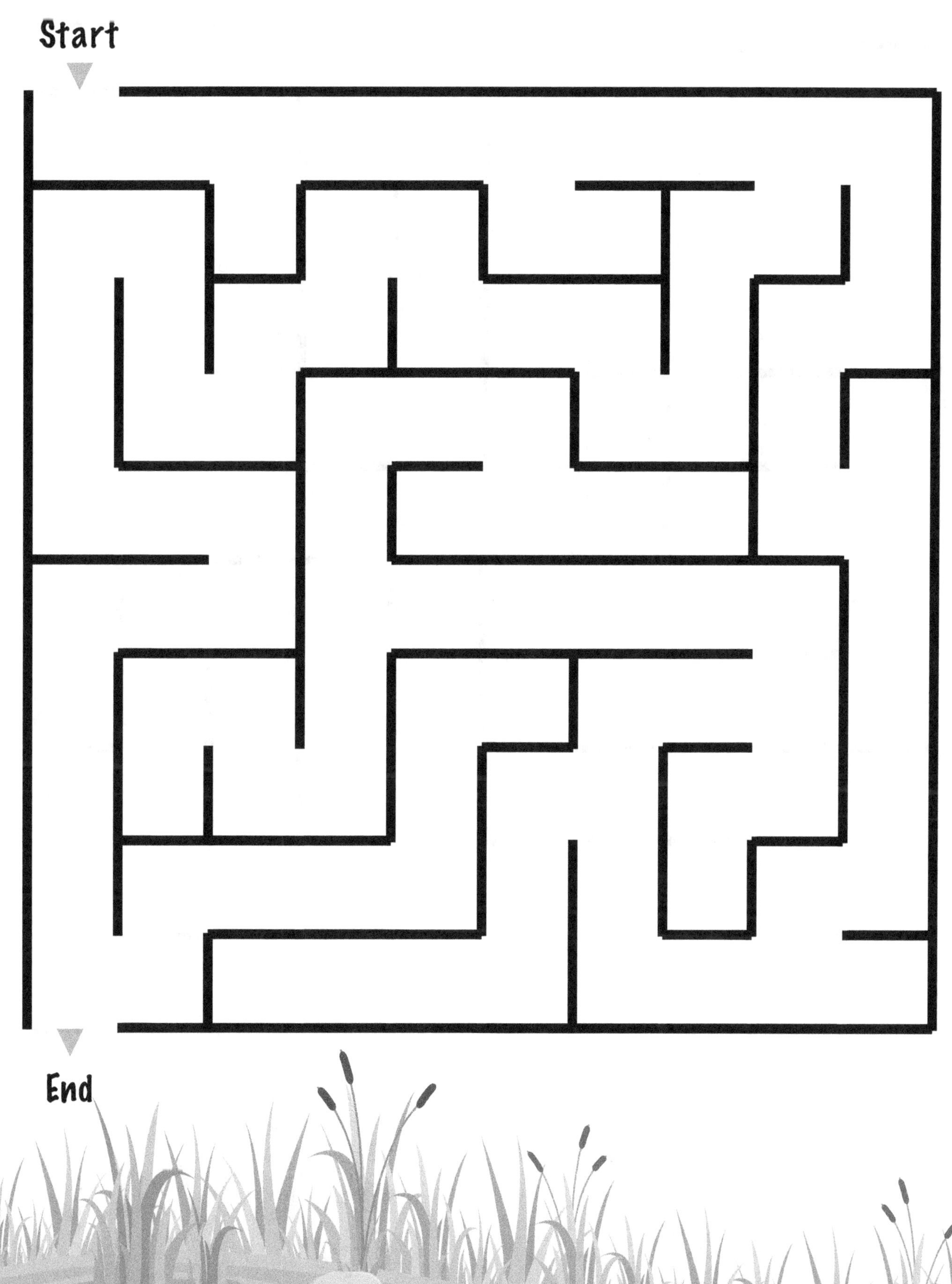

Maze 100

SOLUTIONS

Maze 1

Maze 2

Maze 3

Maze 4

Maze 5

Maze 6

Maze 7

Maze 8

Maze 9

Maze 10

Maze 11

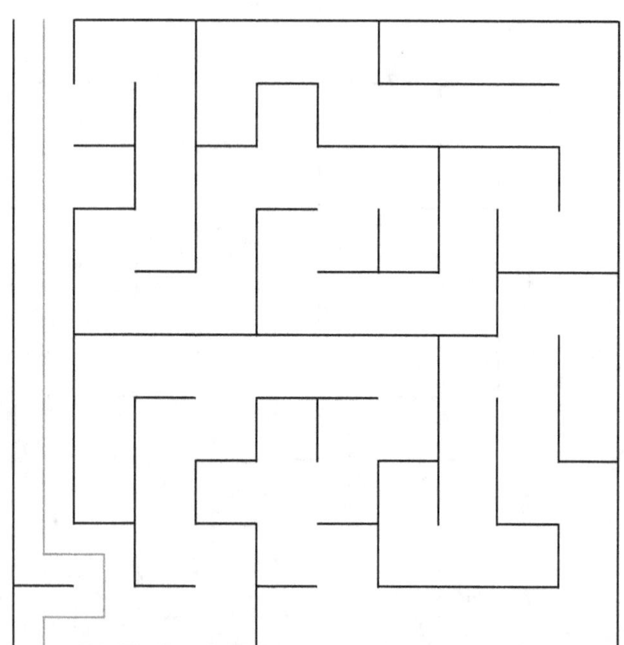

Maze 12

Maze 13

Maze 14

Maze 15

Maze 16

Maze 17

Maze 18

Maze 19

Maze 20

Maze 21

Maze 22

Maze 23

Maze 24

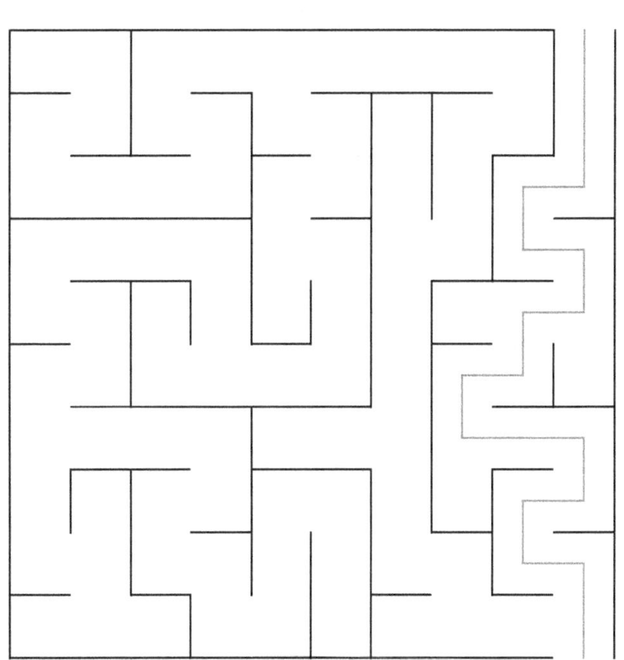

Maze 25

Maze 26

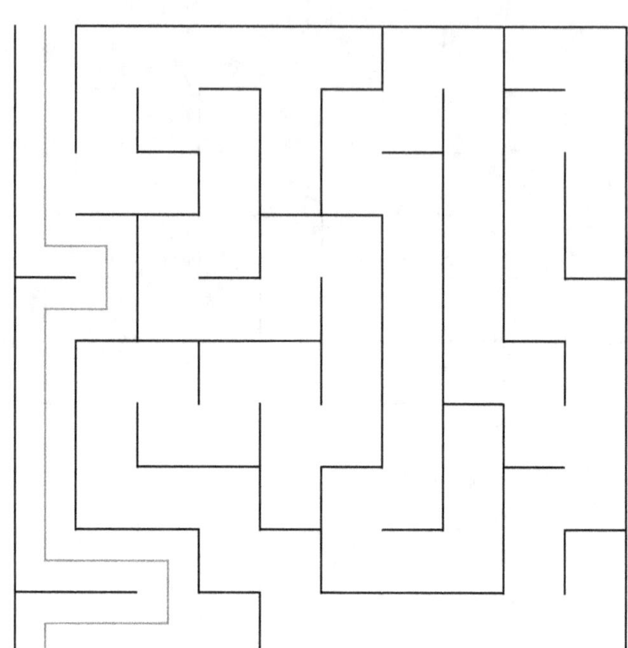

Maze 27

Maze 28

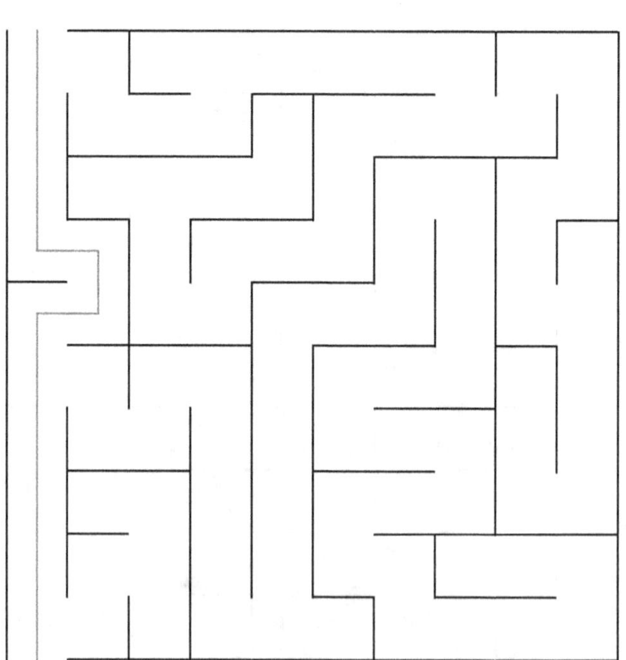

Maze 29

Maze 30

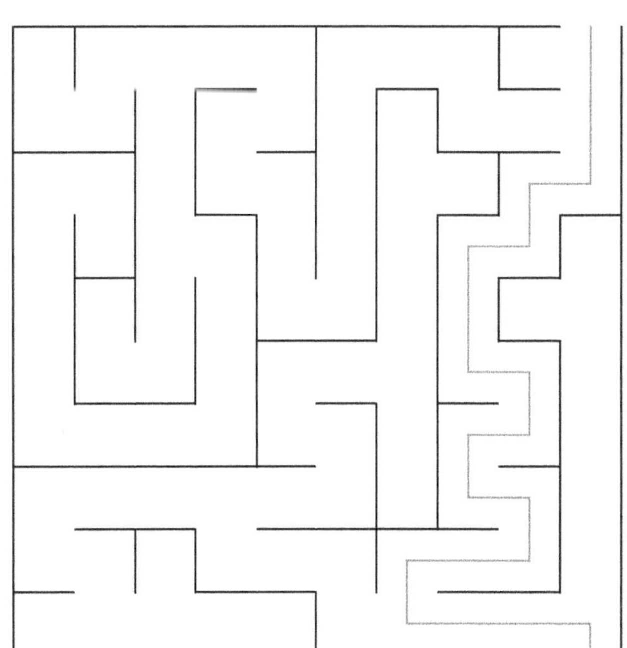

Maze 31

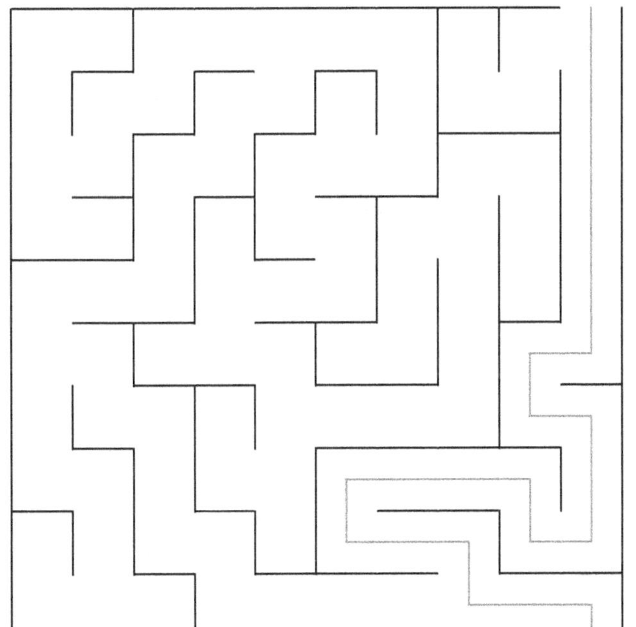

Maze 32

Maze 33

Maze 34

Maze 35

Maze 36

Maze 37

Maze 38

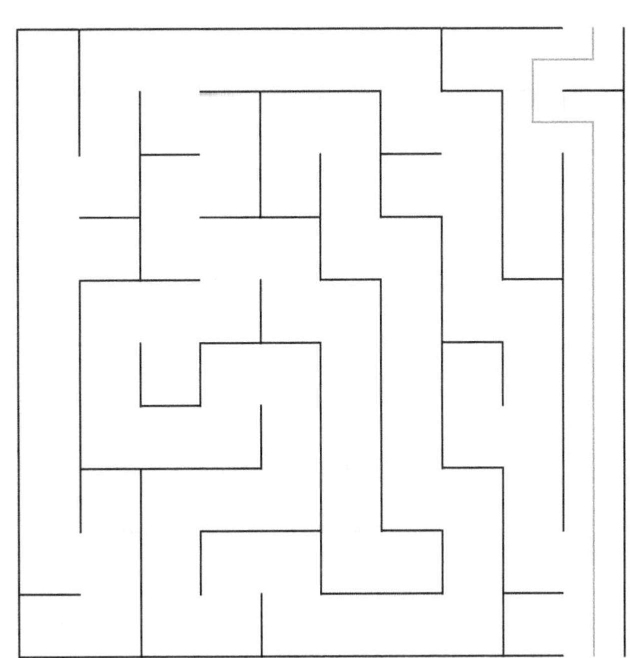

Maze 39

Maze 40

Maze 41

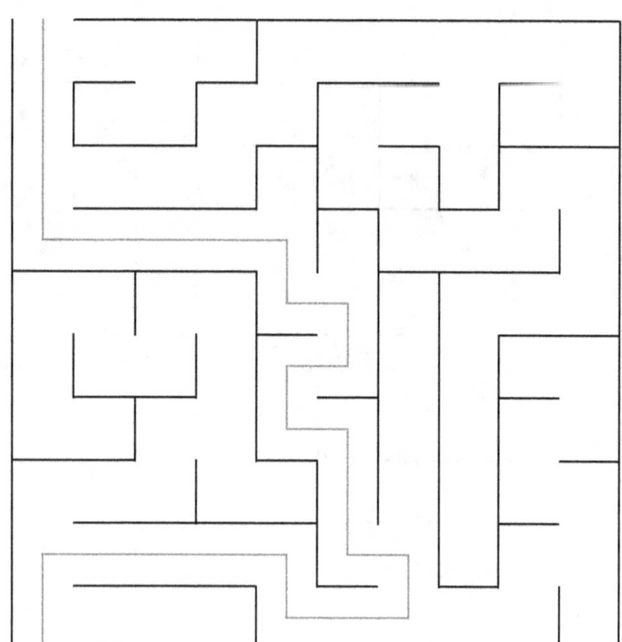

Maze 42

Maze 43

Maze 44

Maze 45

Maze 46

Maze 47

Maze 48

Maze 49

Maze 50

Maze 51

Maze 52

Maze 53

Maze 54

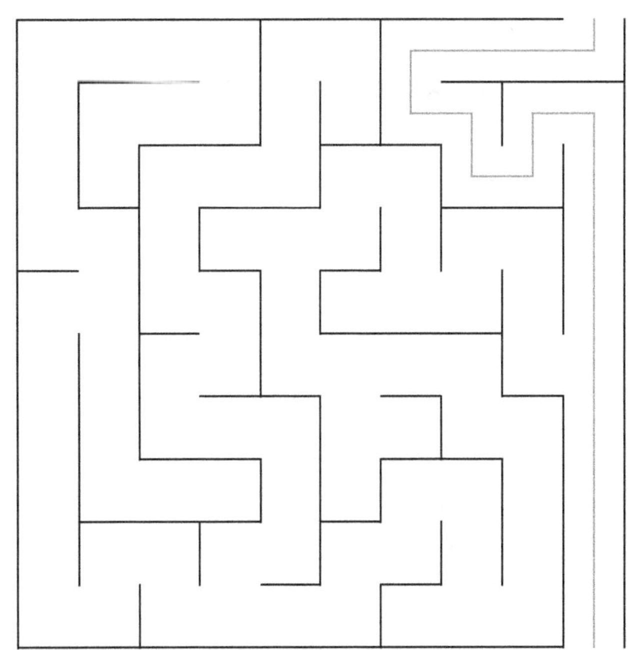

Maze 55

Maze 56

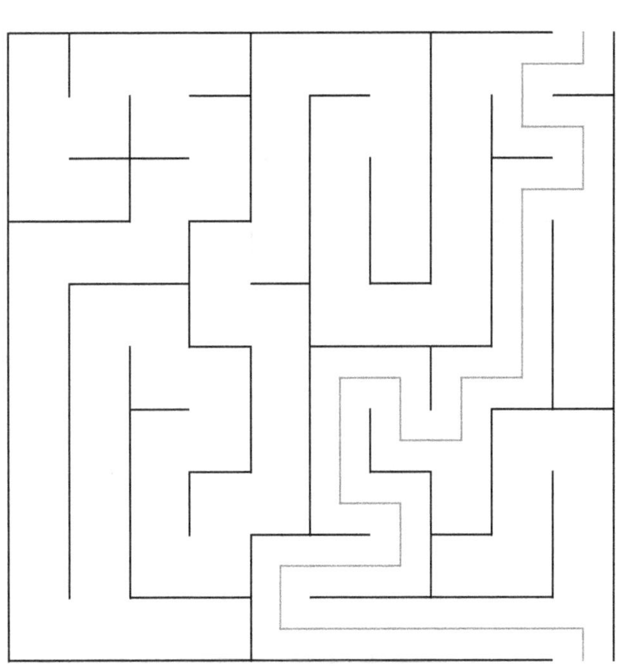

Maze 57

Maze 58

Maze 59

Maze 60

Maze 61

Maze 62

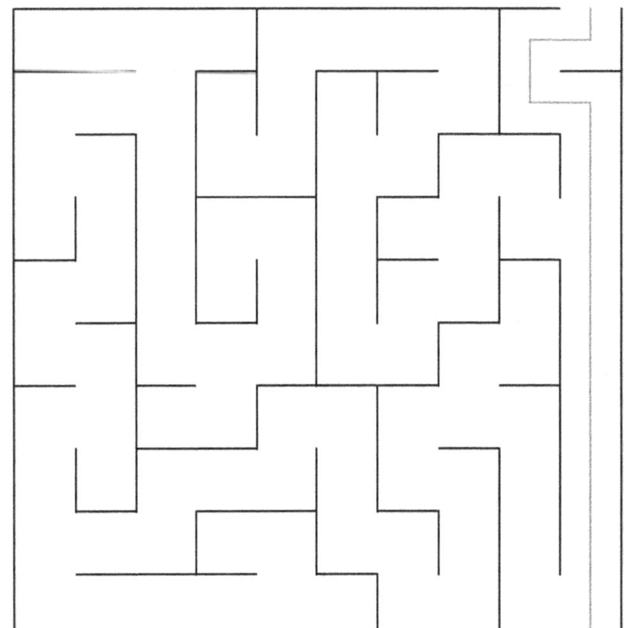

Maze 63

Maze 64

Maze 65

Maze 66

Maze 67

Maze 68

Maze 69

Maze 70

Maze 71

Maze 72

Maze 73

Maze 74

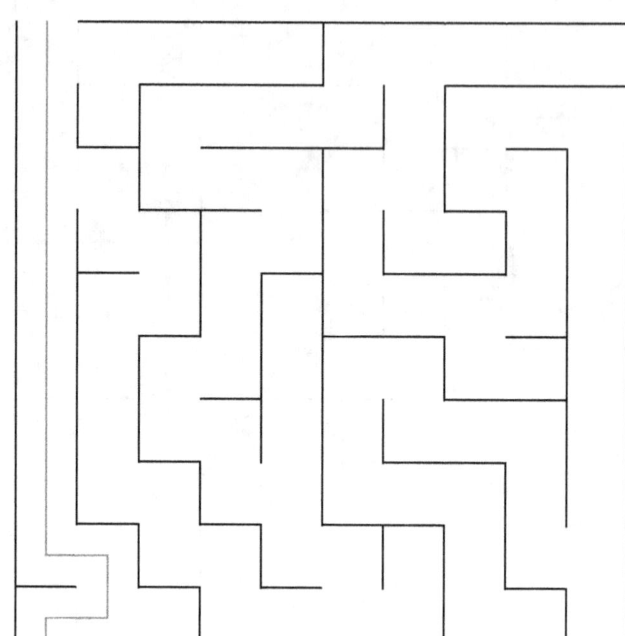

Maze 75

Maze 76

Maze 77

Maze 78

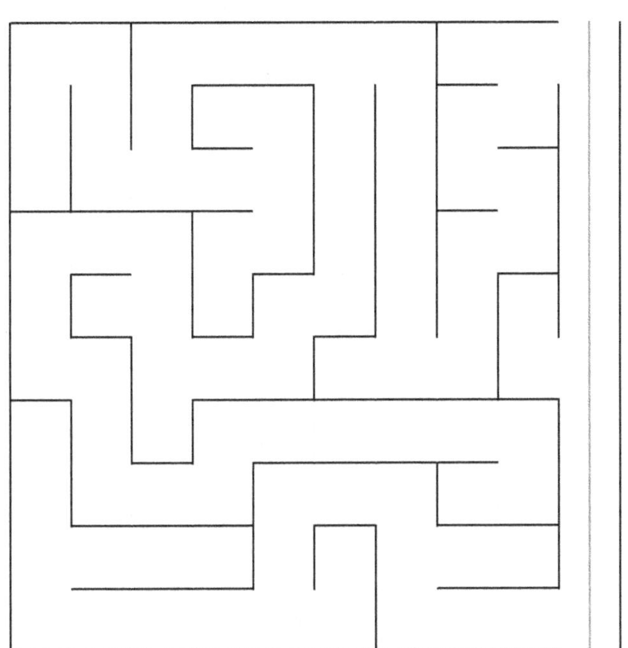

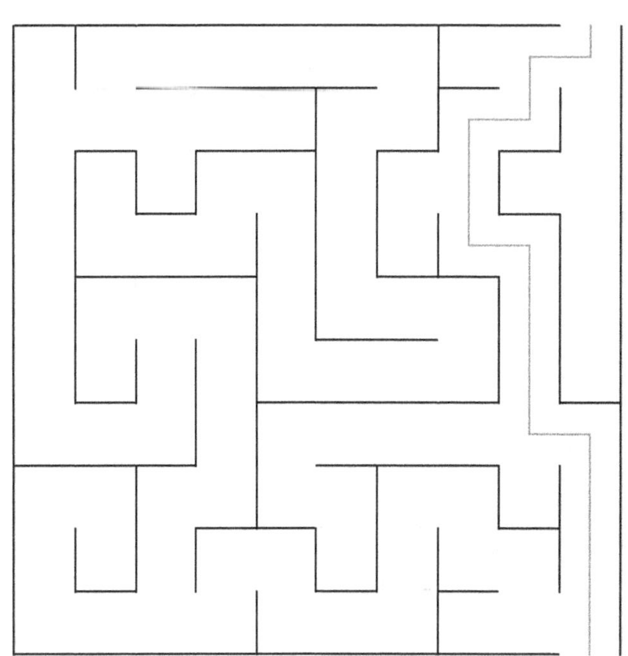

Maze 79

Maze 80

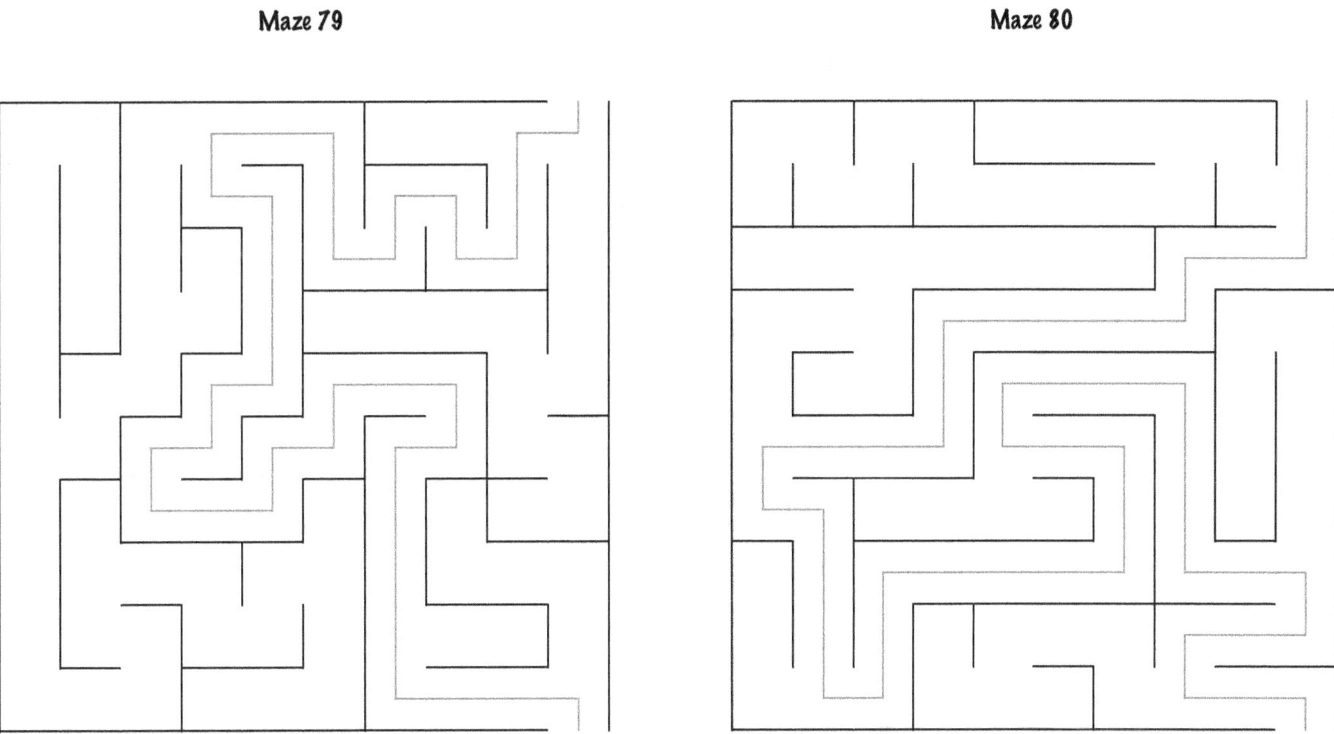

Maze 81

Maze 82

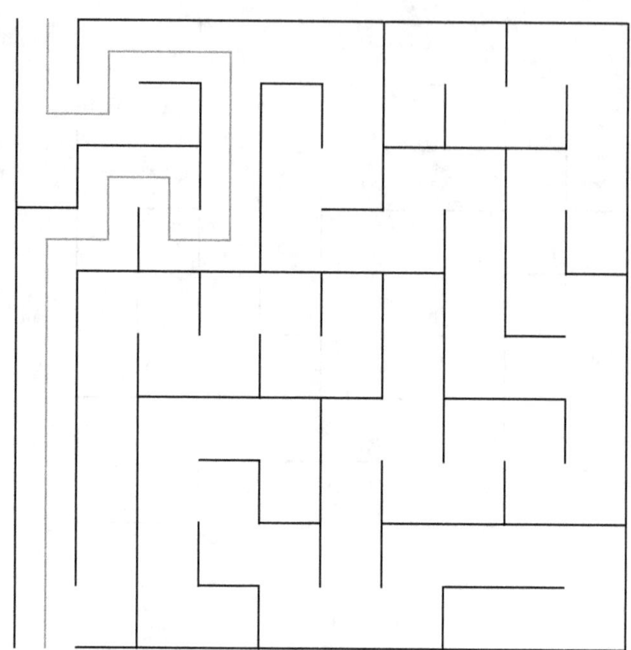

Maze 83

Maze 84

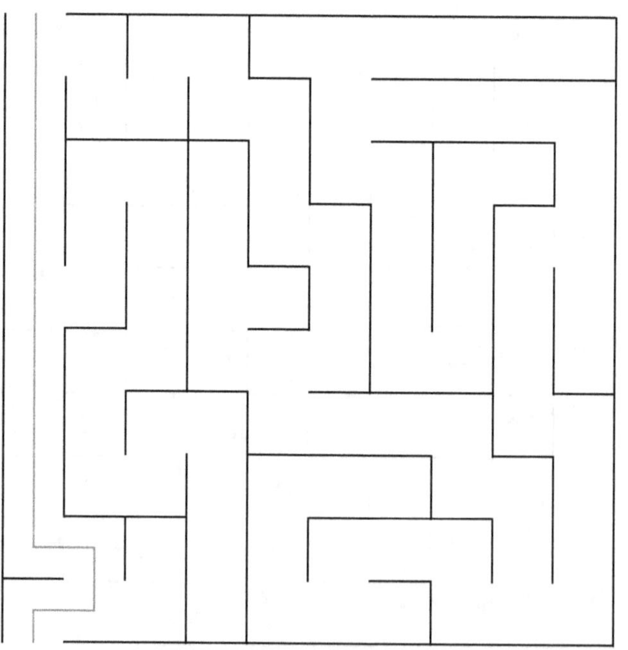

Maze 85

Maze 86

Maze 87

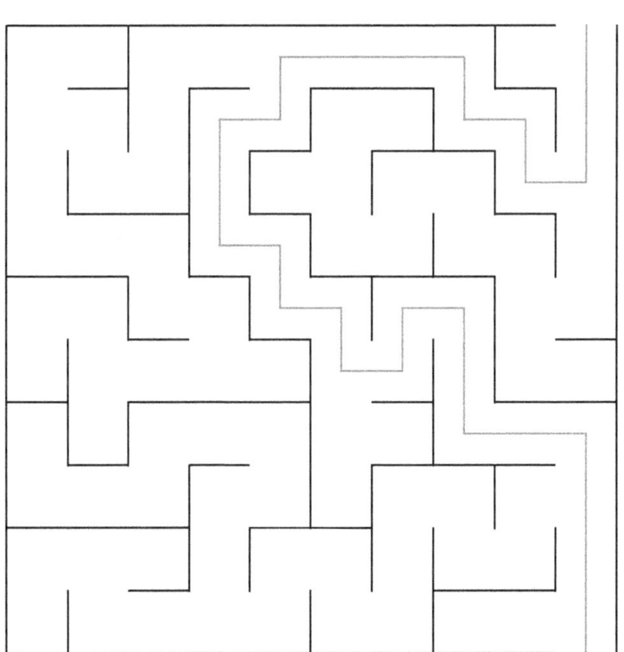

Maze 88

Maze 89

Maze 90

Maze 91

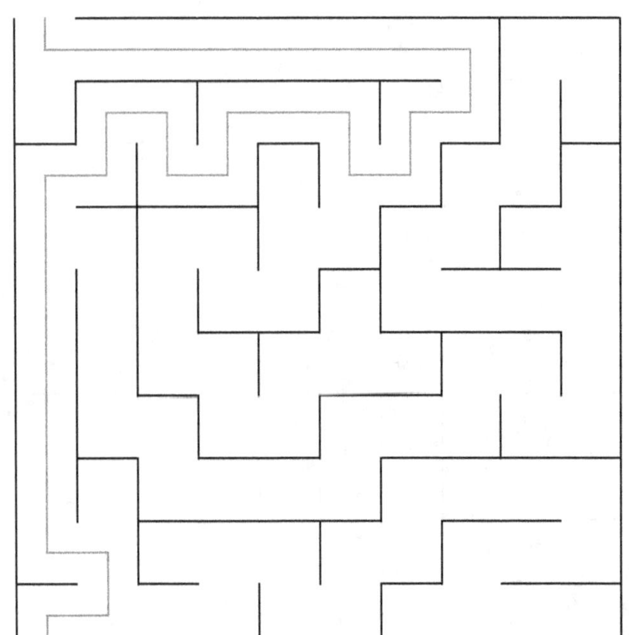

Maze 92

Maze 93

Maze 94

Maze 95

Maze 96

Maze 97

Maze 98

Maze 99

Maze 100

THANK YOU!

Want a freebie?
Sign up to our VIP newsletter and
we'll send you something cool!

www.pixelpassage.net/vip